THE PRACTITIONER INQUIRY SERIES

Marilyn Cochran-Smith and Susan L. Lytle, SERIES EDITORS

Making Space for Active Learning:
The Art and Practice of Teaching
ANNE C. MARTIN & ELLEN SCHWARTZ, EDS.

The First Year of Teaching:
Classroom Research to Increase Student Learning
JABARI MAHIRI & SARAH WARSHAUER FREEDMAN, EDS.

A Critical Inquiry Framework for K–12 Teachers:
Lessons and Resources from the U.N.
Rights of the Child
JOBETH ALLEN & LOIS ALEXANDER, EDS.

Democratic Education in Practice:
Inside the Mission Hill School
MATTHEW KNOESTER

Action Research in Special Education: An Inquiry
Approach for Effective Teaching and Learning
SUSAN M. BRUCE & GERALD J. PINE

Inviting Families into the Classroom:
Learning from a Life in Teaching
LYNNE YERMANOCK STRIEB

Jenny's Story: Taking the Long View of the Child
—Prospect's Philosophy in Action
PATRICIA F. CARINI & MARGARET HIMLEY, WITH
CAROL CHRISTINE, CECILIA ESPINOSA, & JULIA FOURNIER

Acting Out! Combating Homophobia
Through Teacher Activism
MOLLIE V. BLACKBURN, CAROLINE T. CLARK,
LAUREN M. KENNEY, & JILL M. SMITH, EDS.

Puzzling Moments, Teachable Moments: Practicing
Teacher Research in Urban Classrooms
CYNTHIA BALLENGER

Inquiry as Stance:
Practitioner Research for the Next Generation
MARILYN COCHRAN-SMITH & SUSAN L. LYTLE

Building Racial and Cultural Competence in the
Classroom: Strategies from Urban Educators
KAREN MANHEIM TEEL & JENNIFER OBIDAH, EDS.

Re-Reading Families: The Literate Lives of Urban
Children, Four Years Later
CATHERINE COMPTON-LILLY

"What About Rose?" Using Teacher Research to
Reverse School Failure
SMOKEY WILSON

Immigrant Students and Literacy:
Reading, Writing, and Remembering
GERALD CAMPANO

Going Public with Our Teaching:
An Anthology of Practice
THOMAS HATCH, DILRUBA AHMED, ANN LIEBERMAN,
DEBORAH FAIGENBAUM, MELISSA EILER WHITE,
& DÉSIRÉE H. POINTER MACE, EDS.

Teaching as Inquiry: Asking Hard Questions to
Improve Practice and Student Achievement
ALEXANDRA WEINBAUM, DAVID ALLEN, TINA BLYTHE, KATHERINE
SIMON, STEVE SEIDEL, & CATHERINE RUBIN

"Is This English?" Race, Language, and
Culture in the Classroom
BOB FECHO

Teacher Research for Better Schools
MARIAN M. MOHR, COURTNEY ROGERS, BETSY SANFORD,
MARY ANN NOCERINO, MARION S. MACLEAN, & SHEILA
CLAWSON

Imagination and Literacy:
A Teacher's Search for the Heart of Learning
KAREN GALLAS

Regarding Children's Words:
Teacher Research on Language and Literacy
BROOKLINE TEACHER RESEARCHER SEMINAR

Rural Voices: Place-Conscious Education and the
Teaching of Writing
ROBERT E. BROOKE, EDITOR

Teaching Through the Storm: A Journal of Hope
KAREN HALE HANKINS

Reading Families:
The Literate Lives of Urban Children
CATHERINE COMPTON-LILLY

Narrative Inquiry in Practice:
Advancing the Knowledge of Teaching
NONA LYONS & VICKI KUBLER LABOSKEY, EDS.

(continued)

Making Space for Active Learning

The Art and Practice of Teaching

Edited by
Anne C. Martin
Ellen Schwartz

Foreword by
Helen Featherstone

Teachers College
Columbia University
New York and London

Published by Teachers College Press, 1234 Amsterdam Avenue,
New York, NY 10027

Library of Congress Cataloging-in-Publication Data

Making space for active learning : the art and practice of teaching / edited
by Anne C. Martin, Ellen Schwartz ; foreword by Helen Featherstone.
        pages cm. — (The practitioner inquiry series)
    Includes bibliographical references and index.
    ISBN 978-0-8077-5539-6 (pbk. : alk. paper)
    ISBN 978-0-8077-7305-5 (ebook)
    1. Active learning. 2. Group work in education. I. Martin, Anne C.
    LB1027.23.M24 2014
    371.3—dc23   2014007467

ISBN 978-0-8077-5539-6 (paperback)
ISBN 978-0-8077-7305-5 (eBook)

Printed on acid-free paper
Manufactured in the United States of America

21 20 19 18 17 16 15 14   8 7 6 5 4 3 2 1

We dedicate this book to the memory of
Karen Woolf,
Alice Seletsky,
and Steve Shreefter,
three outstanding teachers
who embodied the spirit of Prospect.

Contents

Foreword

Helen Featherstone

Young men and women come to teacher education with a vision of the classroom they want to create. Sometimes this image includes bits and pieces of curriculum: The children will learn their multiplication tables by playing math games rather than by staring at flash cards; the teacher will read wonderful books aloud and in this way help the children to understand theme, character development, and plot structure. The vision also usually includes warm relationships between teacher and students, and excludes tests, discipline problems, and learning disabilities. In fact, the first year of teaching is a conversation between the vision and the realities of schools and children. Over time, novices build a practice that owes much to these unforeseen realities of schooling and also to the original vision.

Only rarely do graduates of an avowedly progressive teacher education program walk into schools where administrators and colleagues support them in creating child-centered classrooms in which they can design curriculum around their students' strengths and interests. This scenario is especially unlikely when a novice lands in a bureaucratic urban school system. When I took my first teaching job, I was given 1st-grade books for two different reading programs that were built on radically opposed ideas about how children learn to read and told to teach both of them, and no other subjects, during the 3-hour block before lunch. The vision of teaching that I brought with me to this assignment derived partly from my teacher preparation program, but more from what I had seen a few months earlier visiting some excellent British primary schools. There children chose their own occupations in classrooms stocked richly with paints, clay, blocks, books, musical instruments, sand and water tables, and writing materials. These 5-, 6-, and 7-year-olds wrote in their journals each day without, as far as I could see, prompting by adults. They read to one another, they painted, they worked with math manipulatives. And they learned to read, to write, and to work with numbers.

The teachers who tell their stories in this volume have developed their visions of good teaching through work with children and also through work with other educators whom they have sought out. In particular, their close and sensitive attention to individual children and to children's work owes much to Patricia Carini (whose wise and eloquent introduction is included in this volume) and to the Prospect Center in North Bennington, Vermont, where for decades teachers worked together with the descriptive processes Carini developed, improving their skills at looking carefully at children's work and at children themselves as they emerge as learners in school. In response to the current emphasis on improving test scores, district and state policies have pressed teachers to adopt new curricula that constrain their pedagogical choices and take the focus off individual children and their paths to learning. In the chapters that follow, teachers examine their own successful efforts to find or create spaces in the school day for children to make choices, use their imaginations, and do work that matters to them, and for themselves as teachers to make full use of the freedom that they do have—what Chris Powers (Chapter 15) calls their "wiggle room."

Teaching in the current era of high-stakes testing and Race to the Top can sometimes feel like an exhausting tug-of-war between the teacher's vision of what her classroom could and should be and the mandates of district and building administrators who are themselves under pressure to pass on mandates from state and federal policymakers. Teaching is, at the core, about relationships in the classroom: relationships that deepen as the months go by, relationships in which the teacher is always wondering and always learning about children. Because vision, struggle, and relationships are central to the work, teaching is a rich well of stories.

A teaching story is, however, rarely *just* a story. Under propitious circumstances—an audience of curious and caring colleagues who have some experience with inquiry and progressive teaching practice—stories support and extend the thinking of both the teller and the listeners. But many teachers look in vain for such an audience. I once led a study group of elementary- and middle-school teachers who, inspired by the vision of math teaching articulated by the National Council of Teachers of Mathematics in the 1980s and 1990s, wanted to change the way they taught math. One participant drove 160 miles on Thursday evenings in order to spend a few hours with colleagues who were struggling with the same issues she was. The group listened breathlessly to her stories, asked questions, and suggested alternative perspectives on the issues she had raised. The effect on her was, she said, "like going to church"—not always directly useful in solving problems, but consistently reassuring and thought provoking. Often she thought of a new way forward on the 80-mile drive home.

Without a group of colleagues committed to collective inquiry and to each other, teachers can stagnate and burn out. However, teachers who regularly immerse themselves in such groups can find their work endlessly generative. Chapter 6, Peg Howes's "Remembering the Child, Resisting Distraction," allows us to see how collaborative descriptive processes can help a teacher to see a child, a child's work, and her own practice in new and helpful ways. The Descriptive Review of Practice, which Howes presents here in some detail, addresses her questions about how she can avoid being distracted from her own core teaching values by curriculum and evaluation standards that focus on "what children should know" rather than "knowledge of individual children."

Many of the teachers you will meet in these pages have found or created teacher groups in which colleagues listen attentively to one another's concerns and stories and encourage and assist in the sort of inquiry that pulls a group into deep looking. This is a book about values and approaches to teaching that are now under fire, a book about teachers who have, through exhilarating collective work, created space for the practices that build classroom communities and honor the individuality of children. As you listen to these stories I hope you will be moved to join the conversation, reflecting on your own practice and the children who intrigue you.

Preface

This book opens with a set of five stories that show what it looks like when the vision of making space for human capacity is enacted. The stories in Part I bring us into classrooms in which the provisioning and curriculum give children room and time to pursue their interests and questions—to do work that matters to them. Some of these accounts unfold over the course of months; others take off in a moment in time. What links them is the attentiveness of the teacher and the assumption that young people's activities, language, and ideas hold meaning worth responding to and developing.

The responsiveness visible in these teachers' accounts doesn't just happen, but neither is it the province of a gifted few. The descriptive methodology developed at the Prospect Center offers a disciplined way to think about the meaning of the many things going on in the work and life of a child, a classroom, a teacher, or a school. This book introduces Prospect's Descriptive Review of Practice, which complements the Descriptive Review of the Child introduced in *From Another Angle* (Himley, 2000) and drawn on in *Jenny's Story* (Carini & Himley, 2010).

Part II details a Review presented by a 3rd-grade teacher who is dealing with unsettling changes at her school. She worries about the many ways she becomes distracted from the source of her inspiration and authenticity in teaching: the children. The collaborative Review process creates a space for her to think with others about what matters to her in teaching and to look for openings for action. This Review is followed by a description of the planning process by another teacher, who is also grappling with new practices and mandates that are at odds with his own deeply held values as a person and an educator.

The Descriptive Review of Practice introduces the idea of teaching as an art: work that is never finished or perfected but, rather, is ever in the making. This idea is elaborated in Part III. The essays in this part form a surround for the Review of Practice, showing the kinds of records that continually inform a teacher's practice and how an inquiry can unfold over time. A Review of Practice is a particular pulling together of a teacher's observations and thoughts, but in the day-to-day life of a teacher it is ongoing documentation and reflection that guide daily practice. Here we see how one teacher's detailed descriptive records yielded insights for effectively teaching a particular child. We are then brought into a year-long inquiry, in which a teacher's questions change as she tries new things with her students and brings materials to inquiry groups that stretch her thinking.

Part IV shows how teachers can connect with children's perspectives through recollection and observation. In the first two accounts, teachers draw on their own recollected childhood experiences. This helps them think about the pressure to reduce play time in schools and the implications of including children's home languages in the classroom. These recollections are followed by two stories of teachers closely observing children who are puzzling to them. Their observations lead to changes in their teaching and changes for the children.

Throughout this book, teachers are "making space" on multiple levels: space for children and for themselves, and space for a vision of education that includes the grappling and uncertainty that have been washed out of the slick programs sold as cure-alls for our educational ills. The essays in Part V bring us face to face with teachers struggling to find "wiggle room" in their daily work. These teachers turn to the particulars of the classroom, rather than generic teaching schemes. It is the specificity of their observations, the power of the particular, that inspires them and shapes their action. It is worth the time to observe and to notice because doing so enables them to see possibilities, to push at the boundaries for *this* particular child or *that* particular classroom. Doing this demands vigilance: an alertness to any openings within the classroom and school, however small, and an awareness of the ways in which language—hence, thinking—about children and schools can be and is manipulated. The final chapter in this section takes a critical look at current trends in evaluating children and details instances of collective action that support a more spacious education for all children.

Acknowledgments

First and foremost we want to thank the contributors to this book, who have kept faith with this project over what turned out to be quite a long haul. Their good-natured willingness to entertain revisions in what must have seemed like a never-ending process is much appreciated. This book began in a conversation with Rhoda Kanevsky on a bench on the Bennington College campus. Prospect was beginning to publish books about its philosophy and descriptive processes, and Rhoda thought that a collection of teaching stories showing how teachers put this philosophy into practice would be a worthy companion to the other Prospect books. The project was set into motion and advanced by Cecelia Traugh, who sharpened the focus on descriptive practice and solicited some of the contributions that appear in the book.

This book would not exist without the Prospect School and Center. Through its school, seminars, and conferences, Prospect brought together a community of educators eager to think together about practice in the ways that are reflected in this book. The Prospect Board wholeheartedly supported this project, sponsoring several writing weeks that enabled far-flung contributors to write and edit together. When Prospect was set to close, the Board made ample provision for the book to reach completion.

Special thanks are due to Patricia Carini and Margaret Himley for reading and responding to endless versions of the manuscript, and for helping us think and rethink its content and organization. Their insightful questions pushed our own thinking further and helped us to see more clearly the shape of the book as a whole and the contribution of each part. Their unwavering belief in this book helped us sustain our commitment to the value of the project and our faith that these stories are important for teachers today.

The two of us spent many work weeks at Anne's house, during which time we were well cared for by Anne's husband, Andy. We owe him a debt of gratitude for the many delicious meals he made for us and for taking care of all the household chores so we could focus on the task at hand.

Our thanks go out as well to series editors Marilyn Cochran-Smith and Susan Lytle for their support all along the way. We are heartened to know that they felt that this book had a home in the Practitioner Inquiry Series, within which we are pleased to have it released.

Introduction

Patricia F. Carini

This book is a collection of stories. Each story is told by a teacher; each story up close to life in classrooms; each a challenge to the assault on teachers, on public schools, and on the work and art of teaching. Some of the stories are from urban schools, others from suburban or rural schools. Some are briefly told, though thick with implication: vignettes of children, of classroom episodes, of a childhood memory. Other stories unfurl on a larger canvas: observations of children attentive to the strengths and capacities of each child, telling the story of how a particular child goes about making sense of the world or how another pursues a passionate interest. In these stories, the reader is privileged to witness how questions emergent from children's interests pursued over a span of a year take shape—more often than not in unexpected ways.

Many are stories of daily struggle to make whatever space is possible for children to make choices, to in some degree take charge of their own learning, even now, even in schools saddled with mandates, with state or corporate takeover a looming threat. Some stories draw contrasts of "now" with a "then" when children and teachers enjoyed greater degrees of freedom. A "then" when children were more at liberty to exercise the fullness of their capacities and teachers were less impeded by external pressures.

The teachers telling these stories have been loosely or closely associated with the Prospect Center and School, founded in 1965 in North Bennington, Vermont. Their stories reflect Prospect's vision: that human capacity, widely distributed, is plentifully and reliably present and to be counted upon—in teachers, in children, in parents, in the community. It is important to Prospect's history and its aims that it began with the intention to join with the Bennington Public Schools. Although changes in local politics ultimately precluded that possibility, the school nevertheless attracted educators from across the country who were committed to revitalizing public schools.

What drew them was Prospect School itself: a mingling of children reflective of the socioeconomic spectrum of the local community, grouped in multiage classrooms rich in materials for making things, a school in which children's interests and choices were key to an ever-evolving curriculum. Prospect also offered spring and fall conferences and lengthier summer institutes as well as on-site consultations and workshops on observation, description, record-keeping, and documentation as alternatives to standardized testing. Through these activities, the community known as Prospect quickly expanded beyond the borders of the school.

Educators galvanized by the school's practices were drawn as well to processes developed at Prospect School to observe and describe a child's capacities and interests. The first of these, the Descriptive Review of the Child, portrayed in detail in *From Another Angle* (Himley, 2000), aims to support and deepen a teacher's understanding of a child. This led in time to a corresponding process for describing children's works—drawings, paintings, writings, constructions, sewing, and whatever else a child might choose to make.

This book highlights the process called Descriptive Review of Practice, chosen for its singular importance at a time when public school teachers are targeted for attack as never before. Peg Howes's Review of Practice presented in Part II focuses specifically on what happens to educating, and a teacher's view of her- or himself, when the surrounding school culture is at odds with the teacher's own values. It introduces readers to aspects of the process, and most importantly, it affirms teaching as an art: a work that is never "finished" or "perfected" but rather is unmade and remade in response to a teacher's questions, to shifts in his or her perspectives, and to awakenings to new possibilities. The Review of Practice calls equal attention to the creation of teaching communities in which the valuing of teaching by teachers is generative of a confidence and a courage sufficient to withstand, resist, and respond to attack and degradation. In making available the Descriptive Review of Practice this book affirms teachers' capacity to take action locally, and specifically on the human scale of daily practice.

A RECOLLECTION OF THIRD GRADE
FROM THE RECEIVING END

To foretell this book of stories and to situate it in a wider history, I begin with a personal recollection from 1940, when I was a 3rd-grader in a small, rural Minnesota town. Third grade stands out in my memory as the only time we did what never happened in my elementary school, either before or after: We made things. We built Indian villages in sand trays and a teepee in the corner of the room. We made butter, dried apples, braided rag rugs, drew maps with names of rivers and lakes featuring Minnesota's Indian heritage. We learned and performed a dramatization of selections from Longfellow's epic poem, "The Song of Hiawatha."

As I recall it, a lot of the making had both a communal and an individual aspect. Making butter was like that. While seated at our bolted-to-the-floor desks, each of us shook a jar of liquid, then passed it along to the next, commenting along the way on what was happening, until the butter formed—or didn't. We made small, three-dimensional Chippewa wigwams and figures to create villages in sand trays on the large, oilcloth-covered library table. We made the figures and the wigwams individually at our desks, but that doesn't mean we were stationary or silent. Many of us preferred to work standing at our desks. We traveled back and forth for paste and paper, with pauses to see what others were doing. When the figures were made, I remember with particular pleasure the fun of arranging the villages that now took on a life of their own.

The Sioux teepee being constructed in the corner of the room and the dramatizing of "Hiawatha" took place alongside the sand villages and other activities. A small group, or maybe several small groups at different times, worked on the teepee. The fairly large group of us involved in dramatizing "Hiawatha" did our planning and rehearsing—lots of talk, lots of arguing back and forth—in the large cloak hall adjacent to the classroom.

It might sound as if the class did these exciting activities for large blocks of time every day. Not so. The daily schedule included the usual workbooks on spelling, handwriting, grammar, and flash cards to aid memorization of the multiplication tables. I no longer remember how the making and doing was fitted around these routines, but somehow it was.

What I do remember is that the teacher read to us daily, not casually to fill a few minutes before dismissal, but unfailingly. Sometimes it was a story, sometimes a poem. For me, it was Helen Hunt Jackson's poem "October's Bright Blue Weather" that cast a spell. After the teacher read it, I read and reread it myself until I could recite at least portions of it from memory as I walked home from school, keeping step with Helen Hunt Jackson under Minnesota's own bright October skies.

At the time, the feeling of doing all these activities was anticipation mingled with eagerness to tell at home what we had done, made, heard. Especially interested in the Indian names we plotted on a map, I studied my dad's road map to search out more for us to add. I liked the busyness of the room, the working out of problems together. I loved being read to. Learning "The Song of Hiawatha," I *was* Nokomis, "daughter of the Moon, Nokomis."

Looking back nearly three-quarters of a century later, the feeling of that year is of warmth and total immersion. Making butter, drying apples for the long winter ahead, braiding rugs for the bare dirt floors of sod houses, speaking the Indian names of lakes and rivers, imagining myself to be Nokomis; the phrasings and words of "Hiawatha," at first strange to the tongue, began to sing, to be familiar. Relatedness: to become what I am not, or didn't know I could be, jars the mind. Makes strange even as it makes familiar. No contradiction there. The words on the Minnesota road map, already familiar, now heard and understood anew. My relationship to Minnesota intensified as my feeling for it deepened. Looking back, I am reminded of the potency of feeling in learning. When a question, an idea, a way of seeing the world, a medium arouses desire for more, the feeling aroused lights its own fire in the learner. Absent feeling, learning reduces to fact and correctness.

In that 3rd grade I was doing what I now think of as big learning. I was furnishing my inner self, stocking my memory with the satisfactions of something understood and fueling desire for more to come. John Dewey had it right when he said of this kind of learning that it "arouse[s] curiosity, strengthen[s] initiative, and set[s] up desires and purposes sufficiently intense to carry a person over dead places in the future" (Dewey, 1938/1963, p. 38). I have never forgotten that year. I never think of it without gratitude.

Why do I tell this story? I tell it because in a 3rd-grade class in 1940 in a small, Minnesota town, not known for innovation, a young teacher in company with children broke the boundaries of the standard social studies unit. I tell it in recognition of all the teachers who have contrived to make space, often against odds, for children to dig deep, to stretch far, to dream dreams, to imagine themselves in other than the here and now. I tell it mostly as a reminder of teachers with a vision of what school can be, who have thought it worth the struggle to hold to ideas and values not reflected in the surrounding school culture and rejected by some. I tell it to say what it meant to be on the receiving end of teaching that is guided by such a vision.

THEN AND NOW

In 1940, when a 3rd-grade teacher—herself new to teaching—turned school into an adventure, the country at large was struggling to recover from economic and social disaster. There are parallels with now: people out of work, wages stagnating, homelessness, hunger, ever-rising numbers of children growing up in poverty. There were also differences. Though the Great Depression dragged on and times were hard, social legislation on a massive scale was being enacted. The Social Security safety net ensured a minimum level of financial security for the benefit of present and future generations. The Federal Emergency Relief Act channeled funding into day care for the nation's neediest children. The Works Progress Administration meant jobs for unemployed people, funding for writers and artists, and educational programs for both young and old that had gone by the wayside. In education, the ideas put forward by John Dewey and enacted in the Chicago Lab School were in the air.

The atmosphere was charged with change. This is the atmosphere in which my 3rd-grade teacher more than likely encountered the progressive ideas she brought with her to a small Midwestern town of conservative bent. Did those ideas bring about change on a large scale? Did what was happening in the 3rd grade catch fire in the school as a whole, setting in motion further change? No, that didn't happen. What did happen, and it is far from inconsequential, is that a teacher with a vision of how school might be, buoyed by ideas and values that broke with convention and the status quo, made room for approximately 27 third-graders to try their wings.

That was then. What is different now are the wider societal influences on schools and education. Attention is focused on cutting back social programs, on retrenchments, on tax breaks for those at the top of the financial ladder. Social legislation, far from being a priority, is on the chopping block. The starting point for government action isn't the welfare of the people, it is the promotion of economic interests. In *The Long Revolution*, social philosopher Raymond Williams writes:

> [If] you start from the activities of production and trading . . . increasingly these are seen as the essential purposes of society, in terms of which other activities must submit to be judged. All forms of human organization, from the family and the community to the educational system, must be reshaped in the light of this dominant economic activity. (Williams, 1961, p. 105)

The enactment of No Child Left Behind offers a salient example. Its heralded aim was to level the playing field by ensuring equal educational access for children historically underserved—poor children and children of color. Politically, that aim was paired with others, neither transparent nor laudable, including as I have written elsewhere "an unrelenting and generalized critique of the public schools in the media and at policy making levels," together with "a press for privatization [of the schools] and an overvaluing of business [interests]" (Carini, 2001, p. 1).

No Child Left Behind became law in 2001. In the years since, the privatization of public schools is in many locations, mostly urban, an accomplished fact. The assault on public schools and the targeting of public school teachers, fueled by political and corporate interests, has escalated exponentially. The now all-too-familiar tactics resorted to include: surveillance of teachers; take-overs of so-called underperforming schools, with forced transfers of teachers; teacher education denigrated with the aim of reducing its scope to rote instruction in the delivery of prepackaged programs; denial of the rights of teachers to weigh in on important educational issues and questions and their own professional development; frontal attacks on teacher unions (and unions more generally), in some instances accompanied by threats to suspend the licenses of teachers out on strike. Lists of this sort tend to drain the real-life impact and consequences of these oppressive dictates. What only a tin ear could miss is the smack of tyranny.

Aligning education, from early childhood through university, with the corporate dictates of a capitalist economic system systematically reduces the purposes of education to what serves the maintenance of the system. Excluded is the democratic aim of an educated citizenry. Excluded is the nurturing of the dreams and aspirations of each child and of all. When profit becomes a synonym for success, there is neither time nor tolerance for a garden of children at play, for hands-on learning propelled by a spirit of inquiry, for the exploration in breadth and depth of texts, ideas, and questions.

Schools driven by technocratic mandates are left with little opportunity for children to learn what it is to be a member of a community, to work things out together. The very language of democracy—of democratic action, of civil protest, of rights before the law, of societal responsibility to protect the rights of those denied a voice—is gutted. Uniformity becomes the undisguised standard for schools and teaching, with federal and state funding tied to acceptance of that standard. The result? Autocratic, top-down governance of the nation's schools.

In these times, leeway for teachers and children is in short supply. Corporations, corporate structure, and corporate language dominate the educational airwaves. Run the schools like a business. Get the job done. Promote efficiency by increasing class size with "top performing" teachers at the helm. Even so, as stories in this book testify, there are teachers who resist conformity and hierarchical control, alert to every opportunity however small to make elbow room for the children, for novelty, for play, for richness of content. In so doing, they sustain the struggle for an education responsive to human needs and capacities.

THE POTENCY OF STORY

As contribution to the ongoing struggle for humane education, this book offers story: as bulwark against oppression, as act of resistance, as guardian of vision, as harbinger of hope. In telling our own stories—as I did with my recollection of 3rd grade—we free them from the narrow confines of our own lives and, in so doing, expand their scope and meaning.

It is the abiding power of story to teach us who we are. Nadine Gordimer cites a story from Chinua Achebe's novel *Anthills of the Savannah*, in which an old man testifies to the greatness of story—a greatness, he says, that exceeds the glory of battle and the heroism of the warrior:

So why do I say story is [greatest]? The same reason I think that our people will give the name Nkolika to their daughters: Recalling-Is-Greatest. Why? Because

only the story can continue beyond the war and warrior. It is the story that
outlives the sound of war-drum and the exploits of brave fighters. It is the story
that saves our progeny from blundering like blind beggars into the spokes of the
cactus fence. (Achebe as cited in Gordimer, 1995, p. 78)

Absent story, memory fails. Memory failed, we stumble, "blundering
into the spokes of the cactus fence," unsure of what we believe, of what we
value—of who we are. Memory failed, imagination withers. Without imagination of what might be, of who I might become, I am rudderless, without
direction or possibility. Prisoners in solitary confinement retain their sanity
by following Nkolika's path—by remembering, by weaving the pattern and
trajectory of their own lives and those of others. Without stories, the human
world is desiccated, stripped of meaning.

It is for all these reasons that "story is greatest." Yet, I notice that while
it is fairly common these days for parents to be advised to read to their children, the reasons for doing so are typically utilitarian: to develop the child's
vocabulary, to ready their progeny for school, to put them on the road to
success. What I don't so often hear is that stories, in and of themselves, are
what most reliably educate us to what might be, to the meaning of a worthy
life, to the meaning of what is truth, what is honor, what is justice, what is
compassion, what it is to cherish the beauty of the earth. What I don't often
hear is how stories join listener with teller and, through that connection,
furnish the inner self, spurring imagination, and sustaining the spirit.

As I have written elsewhere,

I rely on the animating power of story to connect your story with mine, and
both of ours to larger public stories: stories of the era, stories of the race, stories
of loss and sorrow, stories of hope and fulfillment, stories of human degradation
and destructiveness, stories of human strength in the overcoming of stunning
blows of fate; in sum, stories of how humanness happens in the making, un-
making, and remaking of it. (Carini, 2001, p. 2)

It is in this larger context of the potency of story that I understand story
as bulwark against oppression, as act of resistance. To the extent that the
stories in this book enable actions that break with the uniformity imposed
by official policy, they are a democratizing force.

LEARNING ALONGSIDE/LEARNING WITH STAYING POWER

In an essay titled "Slow Ideas" Atul Gawande raises an important question: "Why do some innovations spread quickly and others so slowly?"
(Gawande, 2013, p. 36). In the essay, he is addressing trajectories of changes
in medicine, many large scale. The last story he tells is about small-scale

change, though not for that reason unimportant. For me as an educator it is gripping. The story is of a nurse, Sister Seema, whose mission is to retrain nurses in the field in the use of sterile procedures in the delivery room. Sister Seema is less experienced than the nurse she is charged with retraining—surely an obstacle, and for a brief time it was. Yet as early as Sister Seema's second visit, the nurse's resistive attitude began to soften. Her practice began to alter. Gawande asked her why. The dialogue that followed is fascinating—and instructive.

> *Nurse*: She was nice.
> *Gawande*: She was nice?
> *Nurse:* She smiled a lot.
> *Gawande:* That was it?
> *Nurse:* It wasn't like talking to someone who was trying
>   to find mistakes. . . . It was like talking to a friend."
>   (Gawande, 2013, p. 45)

And, indeed, the trainer acted like a friend. There was an exchange of phone numbers, there were conversations about their respective families.

Four months later, Gawande returned to see to what extent Sister Seema's instruction had made a lasting difference. The nurse said it wasn't only that she had learned new procedures. What mattered was how these were taught by Sister Seema. All along the way, Sister Seema helped her to put the sterile procedures into practice step by step. In the nurse's words: "She showed me how to get things done practically" (Gawande, 2013, p. 45). In other words, Sister Seema walked alongside the nurse each step of the way.

When the nurse was asked what sustained her commitment after the trainer ceased to visit, there was no hesitation. It was the positive effects of the new procedures that she saw with her own eyes. Gawande reports there was pride in the nurse's voice when she recounted her successes. He noticed, too, the use of her own words when she explained to parents why it is important to keep the baby warm by putting the infant next to the mother's skin. What he was hearing wasn't a rote parroting of Sister Seema's instruction. This was learning internalized, knowledge the nurse had made her own—and trusted.

Reading the essay, it struck chords of memory considerably removed from sterile medical procedures. I thought about Lillian Weber's efforts in the 1970s to open the corridors in New York City public schools, to break the boundaries of teacher (and child) isolation. I thought of the advisors in Weber's Open Corridors program—women like Catherine Maloney and Norma Nurse—walking alongside teachers as they made changes in their practice. I thought about Ora Pipkin and Mary Burks as leaders of the Paterson, New Jersey, Follow-Through program, encouraging teaching aides and parents from the neighborhood to become certified teachers by going with them to university classes, by sitting alongside them. I thought about Mary Hebron, now associate director of the Art of Teaching program at Sarah Lawrence, telling a story of how, as a new, untried teacher, she was educated by being brought into a circle of more experienced teachers who, along with her generous principal, treated her as an equal, as someone with something to contribute. I thought, too, about Prospect's Descriptive Review of Practice, of teachers listening to another teacher, relating that teacher's questions and struggles to their own. I paired Sister Seema's companionable approach—"not trying to find mistakes"—with looking for capacities in a child or teacher instead of searching for the weaknesses.

As I thought further, it seemed to me that "alongside learning" creates change that exceeds in both nature and staying power the "how to" instruction and the shallow replication that such instruction promotes. In "alongside learning," change is multiplied: Everyone is changed—teacher and student, advisor and teacher, experienced teacher and novice. In this book, alongside learning—that is, learning in the company of others—is enacted through the Descriptive Review of Practice.

ALONGSIDE LEARNING IN ACTION

Imagine this: a group of teachers gathered to hear one member of the group describe her practice as a teacher—what drew her to teaching, what values teaching embodies for her, how a child has raised questions in her mind about what happens to her own values when the school culture is focused on programmatic change and the newest technology. To tell her story, the teacher uses the guidelines for Prospect's Descriptive Review of Practice, fashioned to fit the specific focus for her Review. There is a commitment to description, grounded in observation, rich in examples, with the aim of bringing the teacher's practice and thinking to life.

The presenting teacher's story will inevitably evoke for other Review participants connections with their own stories of what it is to teach, of what it is that guides their actions, of what it is that may threaten to distract them from their values. In the company of others, each participant becomes more aware of what may be possible in the midst of seeming impossibility.

At a time when the need for action is urgent, *Making Space*, like the Review, affirms the teacher's own capacity to take action locally on the human scale of daily practice. In story after story told in this book, what mobilizes action is not model driven, but neither is it esoteric or abstract. It is local and to hand.

The stories affirm that it is the teacher's *relatedness* to the children, the teacher's capacity to hear children and to take full advantage of what the children themselves bring that is the heart of the matter: a child's novel approach to a mathematical problem; children's questions and wonderings, with nature an ever-present and reliable resource for sparking curiosity; children's delight in books and storytelling and their eagerness to make the stories their own through retelling and dramatizing.

To speak and to act, if only in small ways, loosens the bonds of enforced passivity imposed by prepackaged scripts and tightly prescribed "pacing." To be on the alert for opportunities to make room for the children lifts the pall of frustration and resignation. There is value in any action, however small, that gives a child breathing room—as Ann Caren, a contributor to this book, phrases it, "a few inches in which to grow."

For teachers oppressed by state-imposed regulation and for those preparing to teach and just entering the schools, the stories in this book are lifelines to the future. These are stories that safeguard and illuminate a vision of classrooms, of children, of teaching as an art—of what can be, of what is possible. Educating children to be makers of works, to be pursuers of learning for its own sake, is what this vision is about.

PART I

In the Company of Children and Adolescents

Making Space for Meaningful Learning

The stories in this section focus on daily life in classrooms where teachers are attentive to what children say and do and find ways to expand the curriculum in response to children's ideas. They provision their classrooms with materials that invite interest and exploration. They are attuned to the small clues and telling moments that provide insight into children's thinking and the great variety of ways in which children and adolescents make sense of the world.

The importance of provisioning and choice is highlighted in Betsy Nolan's chapter, "Measure Twice, Cut Once," in which her own experience in building a boat leads her to introduce woodworking to her 2nd-graders. Taking the long view, Ellen Schwartz's "An Over-Repeating Story" portrays the evolution of interweaving inquiries over the course of a school year. In "'Let's Make a Play!'" Karen Bushnell recounts what happens when children spontaneously turn test prep into a class play that draws out new capabilities and sometimes surprising talents in the children. Describing a 1st-grade study of silkworms, Rhoda Kanevsky's "Many Voices" emphasizes the value of both formal and informal talk in the learning process, an important point at a time when children are often asked to work in silence and isolation. Moving from young children to adolescents, "Questioning History" reveals Steve Shreefter's approach to teaching history in urban public alternative high schools, an approach in which history becomes a matter of questioning and of considering multiple perspectives.

CHAPTER I

Measure Twice, Cut Once
Expanding Choices for Children

Betsy Nolan

"Why don't you build a boat?" asked Kevin.
"Right. Like that's going to happen," I replied.
"No, I'm serious. We could build it in the garage. I'll
*   help you," Kevin persisted.*
"I couldn't do that," I protested.
"Yes, you could. It just takes time."
"And carpentry skills . . . which I don't have."
"I'll help you," Kevin repeated. "We'll do it together."

A year of Saturdays and Sundays passed.
Slicks, drawknives, planes, spoke shaves, rivets . . .
Transom, stem, thwarts, knees . . .
Bevel, plumb, fair . . .
Fore, aft . . .

Kevin and I began to build my dory in September. The Rosy Redmond was launched in June. Its construction was the single most important enterprise in my reeducation as a teacher.

Textbook learning was never a problem for me. I could memorize facts, review books, write essays, manipulate numbers, prove theorems, speak publicly. I scored 100 on my geometry Regents exam. I graduated "with honors"—and a sense of having cheated. It wasn't until I built my boat that I was able to articulate the detachment I felt from my formal education. I had lots of information and precious little understanding.

The carpenter's maxim "measure twice and cut once" had to be adapted for me: I had to measure a dozen times and have my work checked before I cut into the cedar planks pulled in February from the icy piles of wood at Condon's Lumber Yard. My success in geometry was meaningless and actually an embarrassment as I attempted to apply simple concepts to a three-dimensional task. Setting angles on saws was an unforeseen challenge. How a miscalculation of an eighth of an inch could grow into an enormous error five feet down a plank befuddled me.

Kevin, however, had the experience I didn't. He also had patience and a capacity to observe and listen. He didn't jump in to solve my problems for me. Often he would wait until I asked for help and then he would wait some more as I described what it was I couldn't do or failed to understand. He had me practice using tools on scrap wood. He showed me how the tools worked, how they were designed, and how they were maintained and repaired. He demonstrated how different types of wood and the orientation of the grain asked the tools to do different things. He watched me as I made my first awkward cuts and asked me what I thought was happening as trouble arose.

Our work was all thoughtfulness. The measure of its success was satisfaction itself. That I had a boat by June was secondary to the experience. I will never look at a set of stairs, a doorjamb, a chair, or a bookcase again without respect for the people whose hands and minds designed the jigs, operated the saws, and joined the separate parts to make a whole.

That September, my 2nd-graders found much of what they expected for construction work in the classroom. Scissors, glue, paper, paint, junk materials, tape, string, and cardboard were waiting for them on shelves that were long and wide and seemingly vast. They also found wood, hand drills, screws, screwdrivers, hinges, clamps, small saws, safety gloves, eye goggles, and a workbench.

Some of them had experience with these supplies in their kindergarten and 1st-grade classrooms. Some talked about working with their moms and dads at home. They asked what the wood was for. I said it was for them to build whatever they wanted. I was going to do for them what Kevin had done for me: watch, listen, and act as a mentor when they asked me for help.

For a good part of the year their work with the wood and tools was largely exploratory. They sawed various pieces of wood, curious to know how the differences in length and width affected the saw's performance. They clamped the wood at intervals along the workbench to see what difference such placements made. A few learned valuable lessons about the center of gravity in their own bodies as they worked with tools over and below and on either side of the bench using first the left hand and then the right until they felt the comfort and efficacy that comes with being in sync with the instrument. They loved using the hand drills to make holes. They noticed that the wood grew warm and the drill bit hot as the work got done. For a while after that, the heat was their goal rather than the hole.

After weeks of free exploration, their educated hands took the same tools and began to fashion birdhouses and sailboats, picture frames and catapults, from the bits and pieces of wood available. Once some rough projects were completed I was able to show them some simple joinery, the only type of which I had knowledge! We investigated the benefits of using screws instead of nails. Hardware-free joinery was possible using the hand drills and dowels from the corner store.

The children worked side by side in a classroom that each day, for a while, became a woodshop, and their designs and products grew more refined. They took note of who could hinge wood panels together and who could saw which kind of wood straight and true.

Each day, time was set aside for the children to engage in their self-chosen activities, including working with the wood and tools. As the school year progressed, choice time became a more critical part of our school day. The children came to regard it as the most important time of the day. We were disappointed when assemblies or other such events caused us to postpone our sessions from first thing in the morning to later in the day. The day seemed for most of us to go better if we had free choice first thing.

Not unexpectedly, the experiences embedded in our choice sessions became important frames of reference for our class and frequently came up during reading, writing, math, and other content area instructional periods. A series of lessons and guided practice sessions stemmed from the catapults the children made. We asked which catapult design was able to throw a cork the greatest distance? What was it about the design that mattered? How could we keep track of the distance the cork flew?

For many weeks a core group of boys explored how to build "the best" enclosed racetrack complete with a series of ramps for their Matchbox cars. They welcomed additional helpers as others became interested. Pockets full of small cars came to school so that they could see "what would happen if . . . "

One day some of the children took apart dried-out markers. They looked at the roll of material that had held the color for a while. Then they asked me if I had any plastic bottles. I didn't know what they wanted the bottles for, but I had grown used to tolerating a certain amount of ambiguity at the outset of one of their projects. Later on the group asked me for some plastic tubing. They were sure I had it, as they had seen it in a drawer somewhere. I supplied that for them, too. Before long, and with lots of duct tape, a laboratory had been established for the systematic dying of water.

The colored water was transferred through tubing from one bottle to other bottles. Varied mixtures of dye and water provided all of us with a windowsill display that changed throughout the day as the sunlight streamed through the containers.

The particular lessons and demonstrations emanating from choice time could have been introduced by me had such a part of the day never existed, but that work would have been more mine and less theirs. It would have felt like a unit of instruction with an attached mandate. Instead, by watching and observing the children work with materials rich with possibility, I was able to help them with courses of study that they initiated. I became the ombudsman, secretary, and financier for their explorations. Their work was not measured by a grade, and yet they attached passion and perseverance to it in a way that made me think about what might happen if grades for achievement in language arts and mathematics were eliminated. But that's a question for another day.

Building my boat had changed me radically. Kevin patiently modeled, guided, observed, and instructed me through more missteps than successes until our goal, my boat, was built. I tried to bring something of that experience into my primary classroom not knowing what would happen but willing to see. What was it that C. S. Lewis said? Surprised by joy.

CHAPTER 2

An Over-Repeating Story

Ellen Schwartz

In my early years of teaching, in the 1980s, I was working in a small public school in rural Vermont and had begun attending institutes and conferences at the Prospect Center. My second Summer Institute featured a science symposium that brought together teachers, teacher educators, researchers, and scientists to discuss issues related to science and education. These discussions cast me back to my class of the previous year, to a multitude of different activities, materials, stories, and conversations. I hadn't really thought of them as a story, much less a science story. It was in the telling, and later in the writing, that I began to recognize themes and questions that had persisted through the year. Similarly, connections between those themes and questions and the curriculum came into clearer focus.

The children were 1st- and 2nd-graders. On the first day of school, Carla brought in a monarch butterfly chrysalis—the metamorphosis was followed with close attention. The idea of metamorphosis took on new dimensions as the children found larvae—such as maggots, caterpillars, and apple worms—and brought them to school to see what they would hatch into. Many of them never changed into anything, but the children were interested in finding out what they *would have* hatched into, had they "made it." Some of the cocoons that were spun in our room we kept all year, thinking that perhaps they needed to overwinter and would hatch in the spring. (They didn't.)

Different things were interesting to different people. Some children were captivated by the notion that familiar insects, such as butterflies, moths, and flies, grew out of these wormy looking things. Most everyone wanted to know *how* it happened, how the larva "knew" to become a butterfly or moth or whatever. Related to this was the desire to see the process in action, which of course we couldn't do without killing the animal. From early on there were children who noticed patterns.

Pattern was a theme that wove through the children's life and mine over the course of the year. In the fall I began reading and telling folktales, mainly Native American and African. I explained how, in an oral tradition, stories are passed down from generation to generation, each person recounting them in his or her particular way. One day I was reading a story—I think it may have been *Who's in Rabbit's House*—and Jason burst out, "I get it! It's an over-repeating story!" I was struck by his invention of this phrase, its power to unite two ideas (at least)—retelling as a form of over-repeating along with the presence of an element that repeats and repeats: a pattern. Jason's phrase took hold among the children, and throughout the year they took delight in being the first to spot that particular sort of pattern and to call out, "Oh! It's an over-repeating story!"

After the children had found larvae of various sorts, I asked them to bring in an insect, or anything they thought might be an insect. The next day we got crickets and grasshoppers and flies (including a roll of flypaper) and ants and centipedes and one fascinating collection of several grasshoppers and crickets and a spider, all in one jar. During the morning the spider got hungry, and the children watched with a mixture of fascination and horror as it began to devour the other animals in the jar. Eventually the class decided to free the surviving prey, because they couldn't bear to watch it anymore. In the ensuing discussion, heated argument arose as to whether centipedes and spiders were insects. This raised a question: What is an insect anyhow, and how can you tell? This became a study in itself.

Around this time, sections of bees' and wasps' nests began to come in. The children used tweezers to extricate dead bees and wasps, frozen at various stages of development. They were then able to look at the specimens under lenses. We had some books about bees, and the life-cycle pattern was familiar from our monarch butterflies. This pattern was becoming part of some children's understanding of what some insects, at least, had in common.

It was in these discussions of life cycle that I again heard the phrase "over-repeating story." Some of the children had begun to refer to the life of an insect as an over-repeating story. As I listened, I discovered that they were using the phrase to identify two different kinds of repetition. There was the repetition of the cycle itself—egg, larva, pupa, adult, egg—which led to questions about where the first one came from and how it all started. There was also the appearance of a similar cycle in different forms of insect life: variations on a theme.

Some illustrations in a bee book, specifically pictures of nests with cells drawn as hexagons, caught the attention of a few children. They were puzzled and commented that our *real* nest sections didn't look as though they were made up of hexagons. Our cells looked more like rough circles. There was a question here, some dissatisfaction: Why doesn't the real nest look like the illustrations? The question didn't get answered, but hovered around us, reappearing in interesting ways later in the year.

We had developed quite a collection of partial nests when Katherine brought in an intact hornets' nest, still attached to the branch from which it had been hanging. We did not take that nest apart because most of the children, and Katherine in particular, didn't want to—it was so exquisite in its entirety. We hung it near a window and the swirly patterns—visible if you looked closely at the outside—became slightly iridescent in the light. With all the bits and pieces and "dissecting" and extracting going on, it felt satisfying to have a *whole* nest to look at and wonder about. It was more suggestive of life to the children than our nest sections. One day several children were sure that they heard a buzzing coming from it! We brought it outside, but there was no activity.

CRYSTALS AND POLYGONS

With the coming of winter, crystals emerged as an interest, particularly among some of the girls. Roberta brought in some crystals she had gotten from relatives and announced that she wanted to make a crystal museum. She solicited contributions from others, and various "crystals" began to arrive. We grew sugar crystals and alum crystals and looked at them under a microscope. The question arose: What is a crystal and how can you tell? This reminded me of the children's question about how to tell if centipedes and spiders are insects.

Looking at various crystals under the microscope, many children observed what they called "shapes." They noticed that they could find "shapes" in crystals whose outward appearances were very different. Some of the "shapes" were familiar from work we had done with pattern block designs and geometry.

One day Roberta found some pictures of snow crystals. There was one in particular that she said she thought she could represent with pattern blocks. She was able to get a close approximation; we had all the right shapes, but the size relationships were different.

At meeting, she shared her "crystal" with the class and showed the picture of the snow crystal that she was trying to copy. There was a lengthy discussion about the shapes people saw in her design, and several children thought that if you "built it out" (that is, filled in the spaces until it became a polygon) it would become a hexagon. Fritz and a few others decided to try doing this with pattern blocks. Fritz continued to work on this problem, but his friends got involved in building hexagons of their own. When he finished, Fritz discovered, to his surprise, that he had a 12-sided polygon.

When he showed it to the class, Patrick commented that 12 is the double of 6. ("Doubles" was a concept that I had introduced to children as a strategy for developing fluency with addition combinations.)

Fritz's friends—the ones who had turned to working on hexagons of their own—brought their designs into the circle as well. The children, taking their cue from Patrick, began to look at them (and, I might add, at endless variations on this theme which children continued to build through the rest of the year) and describe them in numerical terms. They counted sides and angles, and identified various shapes within each polygon, counting those as well.

As children continued to make and "count" polygons, I dedicated a section of bulletin board to this work. Children who wanted to contribute polygons to this board made paper replicas of their designs. Once a pattern was displayed, others in the class added observations to it.

Many of the patterns were based on hexagons. As the collection grew, some children noticed that 3, 6, and 12 came up again and again in the descriptions. They wondered why, and commented that these were "doubles of each other." Other numbers, frequently 1 and 2, came up as well. This was interesting to the children.

For many it was just that: interesting, a curiosity. But for some more number-oriented children, it was disturbing. It didn't fit. The 1 and 2 didn't seem to be part of the 3-6-12 pattern. So I did some work with that group on factors of 12, having them divide sets of 12 objects into equal-sized groups. We noted which numbers worked and which didn't. The children didn't come to a precise understanding of the relationship between the factors and the patterns—which I hardly expected of them as 1st- and 2nd-graders—but they were beginning to see connections and ponder them.

There were some children who loved making the patterns for their sheer aesthetic appeal and didn't show much interest in the number discussions. Nonetheless, their patterns became rich material for the numbers group to work with. And then, the patterns were appealing in part because they *were* beautiful to look at and because, though each pattern ended where the child chose to stop, it also contained within it the possibility of going on and on, of infinity.

Infinity was one of the big ideas that fascinated the children. I had introduced the concept to the class with some simple linear patterns that children had made. Children would point to places on the rug or in the air where those patterns could be extended. They brought up this notion again and again and seemed captivated by the thought that things could go on forever, if only we had enough cubes, or blackboard, or time, or desire. Though we initially talked about infinity in math, the word began to pop up spontaneously in discussions about life cycles, and I referred to it in talking about the oral tradition. It was clearly a close cousin to Jason's "over-repeating story."

HORNETS' NESTS AND ISLAMIC ART

One day some children asked if we could open Katherine's hornets' nest. She was agreeable and became a participant in the dissection. We were all spellbound at what we found inside: a layering of sections, each made up of those cells we'd seen in the nest sections we'd examined in the autumn. Each layer was roughly hexagonal in shape. This brought back some dormant questions: Why didn't our cells look like the hexagons in the books? Were they really hexagons? But the richness of association to the word "hexagon" had changed for us, the observers, since we'd last thought about the questions.

I presented a challenge to the group the next day. Could anyone make a hexagon using only hexagonal blocks? Fritz and Patrick took up the challenge. After struggling to make it work, they finally decided that they had to have some other shapes: "diamonds" (rhombuses). They made a large hexagon using all hexagons on the inside and diamonds around the edges to "even it out." They showed this to the class and, in the ensuing discussion, a child asked how close it would be with just hexagons. We took the diamonds out, and what the children saw was a *roughly* hexagonal form with ragged edges . . . not unlike the layers of Katherine's hornets' nest.

In the spring, the 7th- and 8th-graders put up a display of designs they had made that were inspired by Islamic art. My class was drawn to them, and several children commented that the designs reminded them of some of the patterns we had made and of Altair designs, which many children had been working on. I had two 7th- and 8th-graders visit my room to show their patterns, demonstrate how they made them, and talk about their study of Islam. They showed my class how they used compasses to make the patterns, and everyone wanted to have a go. The children messed around with the compasses, getting the feel of using them, experimenting with circles.

The older children had demonstrated how they used the radius of a circle to cut arcs around the circumference, then connected the points of intersection to make shapes and patterned designs. Though none of my children tried this themselves (not surprising, given how difficult it was for them to control the compasses), I played around with it with my own pattern, and the children were fascinated to watch shapes emerge as I connected points and, once again, to discover our old friend the hexagon. Several of the children tried to connect points, but they were mainly just dabbling in compass work. This was before the days of child-friendly safe compasses, so manipulating the compass to get the desired patterns to come out was not easy. Although a number of children finished and colored patterns that *I* found impressive, the consensus among the children was dissatisfaction. Many started out with ambitious ideas and were disappointed that their finished products fell short of their imaginings. Such disappointments are part of the life of any classroom.

There are always things that don't work, or that leave some of the children or the teacher dissatisfied. I think, however, that there is as much to learn from the "wash-outs" as from the successes, so long as experimentation is not dismissed as "failure" and so long as there is always the possibility of return, of reworking. This is as true of my work as it is of the children's.

OPENINGS AND CONNECTIONS

What I want to say about this story has something to do with science and a lot to do with space and time. I never intended to do a "unit on hexagons" (which this wasn't), or even to connect crystals and wasps. Pattern, which came up in so many contexts, was part of our math curriculum. It was in math that I had *planned* to introduce the idea; I had not anticipated its appearance in other areas. This was not preconceived as a math or science unit, although science and math played a major role. The children learned some information about insects and crystals, but that was only one dimension of their scientific inquiry. Another level came in with their questions: What makes an insect an insect? How can we tell if it's a crystal? Some children got a glimpse into how people start to make generalizations from observation and how these can be useful in thinking about such questions.

Still another dimension was introduced with the notions of over-repeating story, infinity, and hexagon. I'm not particularly concerned if the children haven't mastered the definition of an insect or crystal. So often definition is confused with understanding, a trend that is only exacerbated by the press to raise test scores, since tests are notorious culprits in mistaking verbal mastery of definition or format for "comprehension." What does concern me is that children have the opportunity and encouragement to return to such inquiries, because—as this year's experiences showed me—it is in the revisiting that understanding begins to develop and deepen.

I also want children to have as many different entry points as possible. In the work I have recounted, some children entered through a love of making beautiful patterns, others through an interest in numbers, still others through attraction to an aspect of the natural world. Of course these interests were not mutually exclusive. They overlapped within the group and within the life of any one child. Both formal and informal discussion among the children enabled them to exchange ideas and observations, to see how others were thinking about the matter at hand. Often I have found that one child articulates something that then gets picked up by others and extended beyond the initial formulation. Jason's phrase, "an over-repeating story," is a prime example. In naming a kind of pattern, Jason made it accessible to others, who were then able to play with it, to apply it to insects though it had originated as a comment on folktales.

Materials also provide modes of access. The availability of all sorts of expressive media, as well as natural specimens and math and science materials, allows children to see their own thoughts and to make them visible to others. It allows them to play around with ideas they are formulating, to explore new twists on old problems, and to return to those things that hold wonder for them.

As a teacher, I have the opportunity to see the daily engagement of children with materials and ideas, and also to take a longer view. If I were defining interest only in terms of units on butterflies or bees or folktales or hexagons as purely geometric entities, I would necessarily have an impoverished view of what really were the vibrant themes that brought the class together on a common search, in which each piece was important both in itself and in its connections to other contributions. There's a problem in defining curriculum in terms of units, even "integrated" units; it erodes the ease with which we gain access to the larger ideas by focusing the attention of both teachers and children on x (e.g., insects) as distinct from y (e.g., crystals). A unit implies one, a thing that stands apart, whole unto itself.

I see integration as a human activity rather than an attribute inherent in curricula. When Jason coined the phrase "over-repeating story" he was expressing an integrative insight. There were other moments, some recounted in this story, when I saw children, in obvious or subtle ways, forming new wholes. They gracefully married aesthetics to number, geometry, and nature study. The fluidity with which they moved from enjoying the beauty of a pattern to wondering, "How do the bees know to do it that way?" was particularly noteworthy to me in light of the studied effort we as adults put into bridging the gap between the arts and the sciences.

Connections need time and space to make themselves apparent. The notion that we can teach connections by giving children an experience in art, music, science, math, or language arts around a central theme seems to me to miss the mark. The forming of connections is more fluid, requiring a dipping back and forth over time, drawing on both experience and memory. It defies compression, neatness, packaging, and schematization. What matters most is that there be ongoing opportunities for both children and teachers to observe and wonder and to return to the big over-repeating questions.

CHAPTER 3

"Let's Make A Play!"

Karen Bushnell

Up jumped Jemel, "I have an idea! Why don't we . . . ?" Isn't this the moment every teacher lives for? It's so typical of Jemel—he's definitely a "Let's make . . . " or a "Can we . . . ?" kid. Keeping up with him is the daily challenge. "Can we make a paper quilt like we did when we . . . ?"

We had just finished reading *Anansi and the Moss-Covered Rock* when he made his pronouncement. "Sure," I replied. Well, there goes the project I had planned—I was certain his ideas would far exceed mine. So we measured out squares to illustrate the story. The only criteria I imposed were that they make a border (quilt like) and illustrate their favorite character in the story. The pictures were vibrant. We had five of Little Bush Deer, no problem.

In preparation for a performance-based assessment to be coming soon, I said, "Let's do a retelling." So I started typing as they dictated. "Hey, let's make a play!" shouted Samir. Twelve children quickly gathered around the computer. As I typed, they composed, read, reread, edited, and laughed. The fact that it was lunchtime meant nothing to them. "But we need to finish our play," they wailed.

"No, I need to eat lunch," said their starving teacher. Later that day, the play was completed and the scripts printed. All they wanted to do was read, read, read. And read they did, to whomever would listen.

Something I learned early on in teaching is to listen carefully to children and follow their lead. Enough of my input, this is their work.

I looked up the next day to hear Malik's voice. He was reading the entire play, not just his part, to Roger. A while later, I seemed to still hear his voice in my head. Again I looked up, and there he was reading the play to Que. Still later I noticed him reading the play to Shakia. I asked why he was doing that. His reply was simply, " 'cause I like it." That says it all. Malik, like Roger, is an "old" 3rd-grader, who revels in his newfound ability to read. He is always rehearsing. If no one will listen, he just reads out loud to the room. In another time and place, I would have referred to him as a word-by-word reader. Now I hear him adding expression and repeating and repeating until it suits him.

Shakia amazes me in that, most times, she seems unable to listen to a story, but she listens to this one. She listens to Malik, she listens to Roger, and she even listens to herself. I overheard her say, "No, that's not right," and go back to self-correct. Samir, a very quiet boy, begged to be a narrator. He used his biggest, most expressive voice, making himself seem 10 feet tall. His facial expressions were priceless.

The narrators practice on their own, while I'm working with the "actors." I can hear coaching going on. The children are supportive and cooperative, very different from lunchroom and recess behavior. They seem to thoroughly enjoy each other's company, and hands are purposefully on scripts, not aggressively on people. Their interest has continued for days. If we don't get to practice, they are able to take the interruption in stride. They are learning the value of revisiting a piece of work. I hear, "You know, we should have . . . " and "We forgot . . . "

Most of the children are actively involved. Lanny, who arrived 2 weeks ago, is virtually a nonreader. He seems to have no idea about sound-symbol relationships, is unable to track a line of print, and only writes "safe" words—a, the, car. Even Lanny seems to have caught the hectic excitement and involvement in this activity in that he chimes in during the repetitive portions. What progress!

After this experience, I began (once again) to wonder what really counts, what really matters, and what evidence I need to support learning. I like to think that the children reflect my educational beliefs. Sometimes I wonder. As I write this, and I think about my learning from the Jemels, Rogers, Samirs, and Letitias, I know what's important. Real purpose, involvement, choice, and time are crucial. The children seem to take control of their own learning, moving at their individual paces. They make conscious, conscientious choices. They do it their way . . . "with a little help from their friends."

CHAPTER 4

Many Voices
Children Observing and Describing

Rhoda Kanevsky

In elementary school I was constantly told that I talked too much. In college and later, I found it hard to get hold of my ideas and put them down on paper unless I had talked them through with someone. Looking back over my formal education, I realized that there had been very few opportunities for "legitimate" talk. I knew that I learned best myself by talking with others. When I became a teacher, I wanted to offer children opportunities to think, to talk, and to write that I wished I had had as a student.

I started out as a long-term substitute for a grade 3/4 class in a poor urban area. Some boys were bringing in tiny garter snakes and insects collected along railroad tracks. When I saw how these creatures fascinated many students, I had to overcome my own childhood fears of crawly critters, particularly in front of the girls. We created habitats in the classroom. The children talked about the animals, I wrote the children's comments on chart paper, and we revisited these "experience stories" for reading lessons. I encouraged observation, research, and creative writing. Students wanted to know more about the creatures, and this drew them into reading and writing. The classroom began to feel like a learning community, with shared interests and work, and an exchange of serious talk. School had never been like this for me when I was growing up, but when I saw all the students, including the reluctant readers, engaged in reading and writing, I was hooked. I began to read about education and seek out other teachers whose approaches to teaching emphasized real experiences.

Some years later I was fortunate to be hired at Powel School in Philadelphia to teach 1st grade. Powel is a small urban school of about 250 children. It is situated on a busy, tree-lined street several blocks north of two large universities. Across from the schoolyard there is a small, well-equipped neighborhood playground. The activist families, both Black and White, who founded Powel School were determined that their children would have the chance to attend an integrated, economically diverse public school. Some children come from the immediate neighborhood and the rest from the larger West Philadelphia community, including many from poor homes. At the time of this story, the racial makeup was 65% Black, 25% White, and 10% Other.

Powel is one of the rare Philadelphia schools to still have trees in the schoolyard. (The founding parents refused to allow the builders to remove them.) From the windows of my classroom on the second floor, we can watch these trees change throughout the year. In a tiny garden space outside the lunchroom, there is a small mulberry tree that supplies food for the silkworm caterpillars we raise each spring. Although this is an urban school, my classroom remains in close touch with the changing seasons. Themes of change and the rhythms of nature are central to my curriculum.

The classroom is rich in open-ended materials like clay, paint, cloth, blocks, and sand, materials that allow children to explore, construct, create, and imagine. Books of all kinds fill shelves around the rug area, where children gather for stories and music, listen to taped books, or read and write. The rug is where we join together for reading, math instruction, and meetings. Children's desks are arranged in clusters to create larger work spaces and to make it easier to talk together; I know that talk "primes the pump" for reading, writing, and thinking.

Children talk all the time in my classroom: to keep track, to make contact with each other, to figure out what they think, to make sense of things, to say, "I am here, pay attention." When I began to teach, I wasn't sure how to productively build on their talk, although I recognized how important it was. It wasn't until I was introduced to the work of Patricia Carini and the Prospect Center that I learned that children's work and their talk could be systematically studied to understand their interests and questions and that this could inform me about how to develop curriculum to further children's learning. At Prospect we used descriptive processes to look closely at children and their work. Margaret Himley calls this "disciplined description" (Himley, 2000, p. 127).

My own experience with disciplined description started at Prospect when we passed a chambered nautilus shell around the circle and each of us, in turn, looked closely at it and said something we noticed. After each round the chairperson made an integrative restatement, highlighting themes and ideas from our observations. As the discussion built, a space for thinking opened. Thinking about this shell widened to thoughts about other shells, ocean animals, land animals, and ways of imagining growth and form. I felt refreshed and excited.

My classroom was ripe for this kind of disciplined description. Unfocused talk pulled the group in too many directions. Many children needed to be encouraged to talk, and others needed to learn to listen. Just as we had done at Prospect, I brought in natural objects for children to pass around the circle and describe. I was fascinated by the ideas children had: the connections they made to their own experiences, the careful observations they offered, and the language they chose to describe what they saw. I was stunned by their questions.

When I listened to my students, I began to understand that in their talk they built on one another's observations; the discussion moved in a particular direction. I saw patterns in the way specific children persisted in their ideas, bringing them to their classmates for more discussion. The whole class became intrigued with these ideas and wrote about them in their science diaries. I made decisions about curriculum from listening to the children's talk and reading their diary entries. I planned how to follow up on their interests through more-focused observations using microscopes and magnifying glasses, by encouraging them to draw to refine their observations, and by introducing books and films to provide more background for the study.

I was impressed by how patient the children were with each other; they waited while each one took a turn around the circle. Sometimes, as they were talking, I could hear them figuring out on the spot what they thought—having a new idea, reflecting, and building on one another's comments, or veering off in a new direction. I became convinced that our whole-class discussions helped them understand what they were seeing.

These discussions focused our learning in other subject areas, like social studies and literature, but science was my special interest. This story recounts how a class of 1st-graders learned about the life cycle of silkworms—and about the work of scientists—through talking together. Each year the children's talk about silkworms generates such excitement, and such wonderful ideas, questions, and writing, that I make the silkworm study a central part of my curriculum in the spring. But long before that, from the very beginning of the year, the children are encouraged to engage in close observation and to participate in structured discussions.

STARTING OFF

On the first day of school, many children are apprehensive and also have specific ideas about what is expected in 1st grade: They think that they will learn to read on the first day and that the teacher will tell them what to do and teach them everything. I try to convey that I value their thinking, that everyone in the class has good ideas and something important to contribute, that by talking and listening to each other we will learn together. To these ends, I bring something into the classroom that I love, something that is alive and changing, something that will capture their imaginations without fail: a monarch butterfly. We begin the year by studying its metamorphosis.

From the first day, we look at monarch eggs and larvae. The caterpillar itself is very beautiful, velvety with patterned stripes. We watch it grow and change, eventually shedding its skin to reveal the stunning green chrysalis, dotted with gold. In several weeks, an exquisite butterfly emerges. The changes from egg to caterpillar to chrysalis to butterfly are magical for adults as well as children. The butterflies' long remarkable migration to Mexico, which is continually under investigation by scientists today, adds mystery, adventure, and immediacy to the entire story.

I start the class in a circle on the rug. I pass an emerging (or young) caterpillar around the circle and tell the children to look at it very closely and say what they notice. If some seem to hold back, I suggest that they might say something about size, color, or shape, or what it reminds them of. I assure them that I am interested in anything they say, and that there is no one answer. I tell them that I will be writing down what they say so I don't forget anything and that I want to have a record of their good ideas.

At the beginning of the year, I conduct these conversations frequently—almost daily—to reinforce the procedure of taking turns, observing, describing, making a comment, or asking a question. I read each discussion to the class before the next group discussion to remind the children of what they have said. I sometimes post the transcripts near the doorway so children can read them the next day while they are waiting in line. As the year goes on, they love to find their own comments and reread them. The typed discussions often are included in their reading homework with directions to the parents not to correct what may seem to be scientifically inaccurate statements, but to read them with their children to learn what they are thinking.

Children also record their observations daily by writing and drawing in science diaries to keep track of the changes over time. I encourage them to draw because drawing is another way of describing; when children draw they observe more carefully—the more they draw, the more they see. Sometimes the writing reflects the talk, sometimes new ideas occur to them as they write. Often new questions and ideas come up as they are writing (e.g., "How can the butterfly fit into the chrysalis, when it's so big when it comes out and the chrysalis is so small?"). These thoughts direct them back to do more observing, and we often pursue the questions in whole-class talk.

Our study of monarch butterflies establishes expectations about how we will work together throughout the year: questioning, observing closely, researching, talking and listening to one another, writing, drawing. We will explore cycles of nature by studying the changes in trees over time, budding twigs and flowers, and finally, in the spring, another insect life cycle, that of the silkworm.

A SPRING HATCHING

When I arrive at school one April morning, I see a welcome sight: tiny leaves budding out on the overgrown mulberry bush outside the lunch-room door. These leaves will feed my silkworm caterpillars when they hatch today or tomorrow. I am glad that I took the eggs laid by last year's silk moths out of the refrigerator 2 weeks ago. I collect a few tiny leaves and go to my classroom.

I put away earlier collections (rocks, bones, fossils, dried plants) to avoid any distractions, and make a clear space for viewing silkworm eggs under two binocular microscopes. I choose some samples of eggs and put them under the microscopes. I notice that although some of the eggs are still yellow, most of them have turned black. This tells me that they are ready to hatch. I know that by starting the study now, we'll have time to see the full cycle, from egg to egg, before the end of school.

Each year, I am in awe of the complexity of thought that emerges as the children watch, ponder, speculate, and theorize along the way. And each year I start with both excitement and mild dread. Silkworms will dominate my life until June. I know that once I begin, I am locked into an ever-growing demand for mulberry leaves—a demand that will increase exponentially over the next 2 months. Each silkworm will eat 10,000 times its original weight in leaves, and I will be responsible for feeding hundreds (if I'm not prudent, possibly thousands) of developing caterpillars.

By the time the children enter the room, a few wiggly caterpillars have chewed their way out of their eggs. During writing time, the children take turns looking at the caterpillars and the eggs under the microscopes. There is a lot of excited talk as they look. I tell them to work in their science diaries for a few minutes, to draw and write about what they have seen. After about 15 minutes, we gather on the rug. I bring a clear plastic container with a few eggs and hatching caterpillars. As the children pass the container around the circle, I direct them to look closely and say what they notice.

By this time in the year, children are used to our go-around format and they launch right into detailed description. In this discussion, the children try to describe the differences between the eggs and the emerging caterpil-lars. Nadira says, "Some already came out because some are white. The ones that are black didn't hatch yet." Later in the discussion, Saadiya agrees with this idea. But Lucien asks, "How do you tell the difference between which eggs have already hatched?"

I notice that Lucien doesn't accept Nadira's and Saadiya's assertion. I'm glad that he wants proof. I encourage him to continue to use the microscope and lens to watch the caterpillars come out of the eggs so that he can inter-pret for himself what he is seeing. The next day he uses a microscope for a long time to answer his question about how to tell which eggs had hatched.

Finally he says, "You can tell if some eggs have hatched. Black in the middle compared with all white." This evidence from his own observations seems to satisfy him and he confidently asserts his conclusion as though he had never doubted it (and his classmates hadn't suggested it before). I learn something more about his need to see things for himself.

SHEDDING

The following day we have another discussion during which several children pick up ideas and questions from the first day. I want the children to notice the differences when the caterpillars shed their skins and change from something that looks like a black hairy line to a larva with velvety white and gray skin. The children describe the ones that have shed, "old" ones, compared to those that are still in process of hatching.

They use comparisons, find likenesses and differences, and create analogies with other animals and human body parts. They use words like noses, tails, backs, skin, legs, moustaches, and goldfish to describe them. They notice tiny "horns" on each end. Putting themselves inside this silkworm world, they try to make the strange familiar. Nadira says, "I think the feet are made out of some kind of suction cups." Keith sees gestures like horses rearing up on hind legs, and Mohamed identifies one as a "giant king" of silkworms. Lasitha makes a particular expression with her face to show how the caterpillar appears to be staring. Other children say they look like "rocket ships blasting off" or "a mountain climber" crawling over the leaves. When the children step inside this world, they see the tiny creatures as animated and lively with horns on their backs, dancing along with "pointy, real light feet." They draw on things that are familiar to them to make sense of these unfamiliar creatures.

RAPID CHANGES

The children are excited by how quickly the silkworms are changing and how much they eat. Every day we need more and more leaves to keep up with their appetites; they are very active, and the children are fascinated by the way the silkworms move and how they behave. Jeff says, "They move very fast, but they walk different from an inchworm." Elana later agrees that "when they crawl, their back goes up and then it keeps going and going." Lucien notices that they make big holes in the leaf. Jenna comments that "they start from the sides of the leaf to eat."

I bring out batches of new eggs periodically, so that there are always silkworms at different stages of development in the classroom. This is another way to make sure that the children notice and keep track of the rapid changes, because they have a chance to see the process unfold all over again. From many years of experience, I know that it's easy to forget what the newly hatched silkworms looked like after the caterpillars are fully grown. By staggering the new generations, children can remember the changes that have happened as they see young caterpillars next to older ones. Nadira comments, "I notice the big ones are turning white because they're white when they're grown and the little ones are brown."

To allow the children to observe and compare individual silkworms more closely, I give each child eight to ten silkworms to be responsible for. Their silkworms, a mix of younger and older ones, stay on their desks in clear plastic containers. On weekends, with parental permission, the children take home their silkworms with a bag of mulberry leaves, so they can continue to keep track of them.

Every morning, the children remove the silkworms to discard the old leaves and droppings and clean out the containers. As they do this, they often find skins that have been shed, indicating that a silkworm has begun a new stage of its life cycle. They figure out which particular silkworm has shed. They like to tape these skins (looking like tiny inside-out socks) into their diaries. The children are in charge of getting their silkworms fresh leaves from a classroom supply. This intimate daily care creates a special relationship between the children and their own silkworms.

The children identify individual characteristics that differentiate one silkworm from another. They measure them with cardboard rulers, note their growth over time, and compare them with their classmates'. But there is a fine line between scientific observations and students' fantasies. They identify with and personalize the silkworms as they live with them from day to day. They name their silkworms, attribute particular personality traits and behavior to them, talk about their progress, and share their insights with classmates. The silkworms appear as characters in children's fiction writing and drawing: "Once upon a time there was a silkworm queen and a silkworm king. They wanted a daughter . . . " Silkworms are drawn skateboarding and skiing, or doing chin-ups and push-ups, with smiling faces and hats on their heads. Children set up "races" among the caterpillars to get to the leaves first.

BOYS AND GIRLS

As the children become increasingly immersed in the study and more proprietary about their own silkworms, they take greater initiative in pursuing questions that intrigue them. A major interest is how to tell the gender of the silkworms. What is more significant to young children—what do they identify with more—than finding out if a caterpillar is a girl or a boy? The children classify silkworms as boys or girls according to their patterns and markings. Although I frequently tell the students that we can't determine the gender from the kinds of observations we are able to do in the classroom, they ignore me. But since there is so much interest in this question, I decide to bring it to a whole-group discussion, hoping I can encourage them to figure out a plan for an experiment.

Jeff starts by relating that Morgan said, "You can tell if the eyes of the caterpillar are black, then it's a boy, if it's white, it's a girl." Lasitha and Jenna postulate, "If the legs are yellow, it's a boy and if they are white, it's a girl." Each child offers a different notion about how to tell the difference:

Keith: If it doesn't have one of the black lines on the forehead, it is not a girl.

Nadira: If it has four bumps, it's a girl, more if it's a boy.

Lasitha: I think that if they have four dots on the back it means it's a boy. Two light ones mean it's a girl.

Chris: If it has black it's a boy. If it doesn't have black, it's a girl.

Raphael: It depends on how many lines on their backs. If there are eight it's a girl, if there are nine, it's a boy.

Elana: A boy has two brown ones, a girl has four bumps, two of them are dark, and two are light ones.

After the discussion, the children seem perfectly comfortable with many different, even contradictory explanations. At one point, I try to steer them to research the question in a more scientific fashion by separating differently colored and patterned silkworms and keeping track of the gender of the moths when they emerge from the cocoons. They are serious and polite when I suggest an experiment, but they don't want to explore some future reproductive possibility. They are interested in the meaning of the markings on the caterpillars now; they are convinced that these markings must have important significance or why would they be there?

What I think is important about gender differences doesn't seem to concern them at all. I learn that young children can deal with ambiguity; they can hold many contradictory ideas in their heads at the same time. They don't need one "answer." I read in Saadiya's diary a kind of summary of the discussion, sounding like the loose consensus of the group: "There are lots of ways to tell if they are boys or girls."

BREATHING

Interest and excitement about the silkworms pervade the classroom as many silkworms become large enough for particular features to be more noticeable. I hear children talking about a throbbing gray-blue line down the backs of the caterpillars, speculating about what it might be. Jeff and Mohamed keep looking and looking and, finally, they connect the pulsating line with breathing.

I bring Mohamed's science diary entry to the whole class: "When I look at the silkworm it has lines, and when they breathe the lines get big and small." In the ensuing discussion, Saadiya wants more proof: "How do you know when they are breathing?" Jeffrey says, "It gets visible and then it's not visible. The bottom gets visible, then it's not."

Others have noticed the throbbing vein. Evocative imagery emerges, which leads them closer to intuiting the actual process of respiration in a caterpillar:

> *Joey:* When the line in the back goes away, first the back, then the whole part of it goes away. A big pump of it. It's like if you hold a water hose.
> *Chris:* It felt like rubber.
> *Nuri:* I think it's really like a computer when it first starts up and it goes white and blue and white and blue. It goes between little bumps on the back and it quickly flows to the front, its mouth, and it makes the air go out and the purple line gets it back in.
> *Jenna:* You see the silkworm's body going in and out, in and out, in and out.

I realize that I don't know exactly how the respiratory and circulatory systems of a caterpillar work. Though I have a hunch, I keep quiet and gladly join with the children in figuring it out. What will they come up with next?

Mohamed and Jeffrey continue to use magnifying glasses and microscopes. They suggest that the throbbing line is connected to the black holes along the sides of the caterpillars, called "spiracles" or "breathing holes" in our books. The rest of the group seems to agree that the rhythmic pulsating vein is connected to the spiracles. They assume that air is coming into the spiracles and somehow passing into the "vein" on the back, which is moving in a "pump-like" motion. The image of fluids being pumped through the body like water through a hose helps them make sense of the motion.

Finally, the two boys make an even more extraordinary discovery of another structure within each breathing hole. This suggests to them that there is an internal structure connecting the spiracles and the vein. Jeff writes in his diary: "The breathing holes have holes themselves. That hole if you look really close up you can see a white dot in the center." Their persistent pioneering efforts to see deeper and deeper inside—into the organism itself—expands my own vision. I had never noticed this "hole within the hole" before, but once they point it out to me I can see it.

What keeps them looking so patiently and persistently? Do they have a hunch that there must be something inside the caterpillar, some other structure, that helps convey air into the organism? Do these questions lead them to imagine the whole process even though it is hidden?

They've taught me that deep, patient looking—when there is an expectation that observations will yield information—will be rewarded with insights about internal functioning of the caterpillar. This was further confirmation of the value of giving children an opportunity to immerse themselves in studies of living things and of providing plenty of time for them to observe and to explore their questions and ideas together. I learned to see more from their investigations than I had ever seen before on my own.

I am reminded of Nobel Prize winner Barbara McClintock's work, described in *A Feeling for the Organism* (Keller, 1983). It was through her patient, careful observations of corn plants that McClintock developed her insights into how corn passes on its genetic material. And it was only after she discovered and identified the structures that other people could see them. I couldn't see the "hole within the hole" until Jeff and Mohamed pointed it out to me; they persisted because they had a hunch and assumed, as a scientist might, that something was there. When they finally identified it, the rest of us could see it too.

THE MYSTERIOUS COCOON

One day after lunch, Lasitha calls a few children over to her table, where all the children are observing and writing about their silkworms. Her head is down close to the box. She is watching almost nose to nose with a silkworm as it is spinning a cocoon.

"The cocoon is going to be done today," she says quietly.

"How do you know?" asks Morgan.

"You can't see it anymore. It was wiggling around in there when we came in this morning. I saw it make an 'eight' with its head."

"I saw it twisting all upside down and around," says Gregory. "I think it's hanging upside down now."

"You can't see it now," says Lasitha, "so how do you know?"

"I just know it has to be upside down," Gregory insists.

"Look. You can see a shadow inside, moving around inside," says Morgan.

"But you can't see it so good," continues Lasitha. "There's so much silk in there now, you can't see the caterpillar real good. I just saw it this morning."

Nadira goes to get her silkworm box and brings it back to Lasitha's desk.

"My silkworm is gonna make a cocoon soon. Tomorrow I'll have two cocoons," she says. "It isn't eating anymore and it looks like it's sleeping. Teacher Rhoda said it gets still when it is ready."

"Is it shrinking?" asks Lasitha. "Mine got smaller when it started to spin."

"Maybe it's gonna shed its skin," says Anaya. "It's supposed to stay still when it's gonna shed its skin."

"I think it's a boy," says Nadira. "This one has a black head and two black stripes on it."

"Turn it over, does it have yellow feet?" asks Morgan.

"No you better not touch it," cautions Lasitha. "We're not supposed to disturb it when it's gonna spin or it will come out again."

This spontaneous talk is parallel to talk that scientists engage in with their colleagues over coffee and in the laboratory. An accident, something unexpected, others are called to see it. Someone notices something interesting and comments on it. A question arises, maybe a challenge. Different perspectives. The talk draws them back to the phenomenon at a deeper level of awareness. Collegial interaction in the lab may spur more research about related areas, perhaps more writing and more documentation to clarify a hunch or to keep track of changes. Some of these things happen in the classroom as well.

METAMORPHOSIS

By the time we sit down together in early June, most, but not all, of the caterpillars have made cocoons. Some moths have emerged already, but the children are waiting for the others. I realize that this is a good time to discuss the question that I noticed in Morgan's journal a couple of weeks ago: "And how do they turn into a moth?" On the same day, Chris had drawn a picture of a silkworm with antennae. We both laughed about his picture. But it made me wonder what ideas were forming about the process of metamorphosis. I knew the children often looked at pictures that showed the changes going on inside the cocoon, and I had cut open several cocoons from the year before to show them that the real thing looks just like the pictures (or vice versa). In each cocoon we find the old wrinkled-up skin that the caterpillar shed when it changed into a pupal form inside the cocoon. I am curious to hear what the children imagine is happening.

> *Teacher Rhoda:* People were saying that they wonder what happens inside the cocoon. What do you think?
> *Mohamed:* In the cocoon, the face stays the same. The legs get smaller and maybe on his back he grows wings and when he finally comes out of the cocoon, the wings are half out and his body isn't.

Keith: Maybe he sheds one more time in the cocoon, then the skin turns into wings and the antennas sprout. And they got less legs and one long leg in front on each side.

Jeff: When they're in the cocoon, they shed one more time before they turn into moths.

Anaya: When you wasn't here and we came back, all the silkworms were big. The boys were saying, "Cool!" The girls were saying, "Wow!"

Jenna: I was thinking, what happened to the breathing holes when they are moths?

Joey: I didn't know what Mohamed meant, by the legs get smaller. They get longer though.

Raphael: The breathing holes suck into their bodies, that's how they can breathe through their noses. The wings just come out their body. The antennas get real, real long and the face changes.

Chris: I draw the silkworms with antennas. I kind of shape out the shape of the moth on the silkworm. I mean I make a silkworm with antennas.

Lucien: Well, some people think they eat clothes. They don't. They see moths, they say, the moth ate the clothes. But that really didn't happen.

Iris: That they eat a lot. And grow and make cocoons.

Jackie: When they make cocoons, they make moths.

Shantell: When they are in the cocoon, Lucien said that they change. And their feet change into the wings.

Lucien: The silkworm skin stays the same, the rest of the body changes.

Nadira: Something like Shantell. I think the breathing holes—inside the breathing holes it's just like tiny feathers. Say the antennas are all split up. Each one a feather inside the breathing holes—one little feather comes out of the breathing holes and comes together and makes one. On each side the same thing.

I am fascinated by the children's imaginative ways of accounting for the dramatic change of body form that they have witnessed. I notice that they are trying to come up with explanations of how this may have happened and how the new form relates to the old one. Even Chris's playful drawing was done by superimposing the shape of the moth on the silkworm. I can see that our intensive study of the caterpillars' breathing holes is now stimulating speculation about what became of the breathing holes and how moths breathe.

Nadira has the notion that the raw materials for the moth are within the caterpillar from the beginning, although you only have a faint glimmer of them. Although she doesn't know what makes it possible to have continuity across generations—what determines how a child grows up and resembles its parent—she imagines that a caterpillar is set up from the first to become a moth and not something else. The research I did informed me that there are imaginal cells, dormant in the caterpillar, which become active within the pupa when the structures of the caterpillar break down. These cells make possible the chemical interactions that will result in new structures that make up the moth. Nadira doesn't know about these cells or about genes and what directs growth and change. But she speculates that the pieces that make up the adult—the feathers that will become the antennae—exist from the beginning in the larval form. The blueprint for the adult is invisible, but it is there; continuity is maintained within an organism although it totally changes its form.

THE CIRCLE OF LIFE

When children are given time and space for close observation, they can make remarkable discoveries, such as Mohamed's and Jeffrey's about how caterpillar respiration works. They can also come to sophisticated insights, such as Nadira's thoughts about continuity across generations. Our class discussions provide the means for children to share observations and to revisit experiences, questions, and ideas. By talking together, children build on each other's thinking and push it further.

I have learned by listening to children and talking with them that even very young children are complex thinkers, capable of connecting ideas from wide-ranging realms of their experience and memory. As a final comment after all the talk about which silkworms are boys and which ones are girls, Elana says:

> It's just like the way we had the butterfly. First they caterpillars. Then they turn into cocoons. Then the moth comes out. Then they mate. Then they lay eggs and die. And children do what they do. It goes over and over—like us. First you're a grown-up and the lady has a baby and then the baby grows to a grown-up. Like the silkworm. It's called the circle of life.

CHAPTER 5

Questioning History

Steve Shreefter
(In conversation with Ellen Schwartz)

Steve Shreefter, who taught high school in New York City until retiring in 2007, attended
Prospect Summer Institutes from 1998 to 2010. There he met Ellen Schwartz, an
elementary teacher from Vermont. One summer they got into a conversation about the
testing mandates that have overtaken public education. Steve explained how he prepared
high school students for the standardized history tests while working with them to develop
an understanding of ideological perspective in U.S. history and government. In 2007, Ellen
asked Steve if she could interview him about this work. She started by asking Steve about
his own teaching history.

Steve: For 28 years, beginning in 1979, I worked in the New York City
school system, almost exclusively in the public alternative high
schools. Most of those original alternative schools have been phased
out or redesigned. The first alternative high schools were often seen
as dumping grounds for kids from the larger schools. Some of the
students at Bronx Regional High School in the South Bronx had been
in six or seven or eight different high schools. Many were older, and
although they'd been in so many schools, they had very few credits.
So, for many kids, Regional was their last hope for graduating.

Ellen: When did you work at Bronx Regional?

Steve: I got there in 1981 and stayed for 14 years. At Regional, we tried
to make coming back to school comfortable for the older kids. They
received credits for their courses, but weren't labeled as "freshmen"
or "sophomores." Students could stay until their 22nd birthday. Now
it's changed. It's harder and harder to find places that admit students
who need to be in a new setting. A 17-year-old who doesn't have a
substantial number of the credits they need to graduate won't be able
to enter an alternative school. They're told to get a GED.

The alternative schools were smaller, more personalized, and didn't have the pressure of the state tests. That was a boon to kids who were coming from large, comprehensive high schools, where they were required to take New York State Regents exams. Students were having trouble passing those tests. For many kids, the alternative schools were places where they could come, feel that they were seen and heard, and not be in classes that were mainly test prep.

In the middle 1980s students at alternative high schools had to start taking state tests like the Regents exams, which were called the Regents Competency Tests (RCTs). If they passed all the RCT exams, they would get a diploma, but it wasn't a Regents Diploma, like the kids in the more academic high schools. In hindsight, it was the beginning of the state's mandate to test all children. At some point, the RCTs were eliminated for all but special education. Now all students are required to take Regents exams in every subject except electives. There are only a few schools that have waivers for some of those tests. So the testing mandate has escalated in terms of type of tests and the number of tests. We started testing early. It was never ending. We tried to get high school students to pass all the tests as soon as possible, because they were required for graduation.

At Bronx Regional, graduation was very meaningful for our students. Many kids never thought they would graduate. They were older. Some were parents. We had a large number of teen mothers. We even had a child care center. Kids needed to graduate in order to get on with their lives. So the test became a real concern, something many alternative school teachers wanted to ignore, to say, "How dare they? This is an alternative school. We're going to ignore these." But we couldn't.

I worked with a group of teachers. We always varied our curriculum, redoing it and replanning it. It changed from year to year, semester to semester, day to day, and class to class in terms of the issues we thought were important and how we taught. For me the question became how to continue teaching in a way that made sense for me and the students but also prepared students to pass the test. How could I take something that both teachers and kids didn't want to do—test prep—and make it an experience that went beyond just that? How could I turn it on its head?

Finally, I realized you could actually spend a period of time *just before* the test preparing the kids to take it. So that's the approach that I developed, and it worked. It was a challenge.

Ellen: So let's go back. How did you conceive of your job as a teacher of history? How did you teach history before you started prepping the students for the tests?

Steve: It's a particular challenge to teach something when the kids have
had an experience that turns them off. I don't know how many times
I've heard kids say, "I hate history." The problem is, of course, that
for many kids—and for many of us—history is really about someone
else. It doesn't really answer any of our authentic questions. Also,
it's often taught in a way that doesn't *raise* any questions. History is
seen as something static that's been handed down. Not as a living,
breathing process, which allows you to connect yourself to the
world. It's taught as the agreed-upon story. For immigrants, it's the
Americanizing story. Some kids learn it; they pass and move on. But
most of the kids I've taught are more sassy and less willing to sit
back and agree. They probably have more questions and often are
thinking—whether consciously, unconsciously or intuitively—that
what they know about their own lives, their own histories, their own
families, and their own neighborhoods has nothing to do with the
history in textbooks.

It's like when I was in 3rd grade and for the 18th time they were
telling us about our forefathers who came on the *Mayflower*. I was
sitting in this classroom in Brooklyn, and it dawned on me that they
weren't talking about me. My mind flashed to my grandmother Zelda,
who spoke with a thick Eastern European accent. I realized that
she didn't speak with a British accent. It was an epiphany that the
story these people were telling had nothing to do with me. It got me
thinking. And the gap was not as great for me, in an all-White school,
a segregated elementary school, as for the kids I teach who are not
from a European background.

As a history teacher, I didn't see my job as "covering" the Era
of Good Feeling, and then the Civil War, and the Gilded Age, and
the Roaring 20s. Instead I wanted to show how all these things are
connected, that there are larger social and economic forces at play. I
believe that having some understanding about this allows you to see
the connections.

Ellen: Could you give an example of how you've done this with kids?

Steve: It varied. Sometimes we would look at what they knew of their
city or state or country today and try to identify issues that were
problematic, the questions they had, and try to find their roots. So kids
would talk about—especially in the South Bronx—issues of poverty,
issues of poor education. Then we would try to figure out how we
got to be there. We took all the kids and we plotted when their family
either migrated or immigrated. We made a graph. My grandparents
came from Eastern Europe and I was part of *that* migration. There
were Puerto Rican kids who could trace their families' arrival to the
Puerto Rican migration of the 1950s. And there was the more recent

migration from the Dominican Republic. Then we could see that we all had individual stories but were part of larger historical movements.

When I worked at the Urban Academy, I taught an oral history class. We looked at the civil rights movement and the Vietnam War. Kids went home and interviewed relatives who were alive at the time, though not necessarily politically active. I brought in people so the kids could interview them. It also gave the class the opportunity to transcribe and talk about accuracy. There were differences in what people heard.

At Regional, I used oral histories as well. We went to a senior citizen lunch program when we were studying the bombing of Hiroshima and Nagasaki. These people had all lived through that. They were mainly African American. Amazing things happened. You can't plan for this. A young woman started interviewing this man, and he said, "Oh, I was in the war. I fought in World War II. I was in a segregated Army unit." This raised the phenomenon of segregation in the Army. And here was a guy who gave us beautiful descriptions of northern Africa and his experiences. It allowed the kids to start at a particular place with particular questions, and then open up new questions about issues that came up.

With earlier historical periods, like the Civil War, I brought in videotapes so kids would have visual images and could imagine it. I used documentation, references, primary sources, and novels—so it would be alive even though there was no one alive from that period of time.

Ellen: When you were talking about the interviews, you said it brought up issues of accuracy. What kinds of issues came up?

Steve: It was interesting. There was the person him- or herself who saw a particular event. Then if we had a number of interviews about that event, the students would see that there were multiple perspectives, based on vantage point and prior experience. That was one question: How come six people lived through an event and there were different interpretations? Sometimes I would bring someone into the classroom and not use a tape, purposely. I would ask kids to take notes and write up the interview in the first person, as if that person were speaking. So the issue of accuracy would come up. There were significant contradictions among the transcriptions, which meant that we had heard it differently. Sometimes we weren't listening very well or we couldn't read our writing, but somehow in the process of hearing someone and filtering it, it was hard to separate what the person had said from our own experiences and how we heard it. Of course, that could lead to questions about accuracy in textbooks.

Ellen: When the kids studied about the Civil War and couldn't interview people, were there ways you could draw on their experience in interviewing to help them think about how the sources they were looking at also had to be from a perspective?

Steve: If you're interviewing someone and you say it's a transcription, then you want to be as accurate as possible. But if you're looking at history, pretty soon you know that there are multiple perspectives and, in fact, it's hard to say one is right and one is wrong. We may disagree with an author's worldview, but part of understanding history—people in time and place—is understanding how they get to that worldview and how worldviews can be so different.

So that was one goal: to get kids thinking about history, being interested in it, knowing that they could ferret it out. And then to further understand that we and people we know make history. Martin Luther King is the person we read about in the textbook. But he wouldn't have been so well known if it hadn't been for all those women whose names we'll never know—the thousands of women who organized the bus boycott, who organized the carpools, who did all the leafleting. They made history. I always said, "Interview someone who lived through it, active or not, because people are influenced by the time they live in."

There are parallels to the kids' lives. They are living in a particular time, with particular feelings about things. So the kids in my previous school—some were born here, some not—and the word "immigrant" is used as a curse word. Kids get mad at each other and say, "You immigrant." They didn't invent that. It comes directly from the current anti-immigrant feeling. When I say that to kids, they sometimes stop and realize that they're repeating something that's actually hostile to them and their families and that devalues their own history. Those were some of the issues that I've taught, connecting kids with their own authentic history and the contributions that working people made, often their parents and grandparents: why people immigrate to the United States, what they do when they get here, their expectations, what they find, and how people change things and make history. The ideal would be to have kids for longer periods of time, really doing historical research.

Ellen: It sounds like they were doing some of it when they were doing interviews.

Steve: They were. Those are the high moments. Then there was also the tape where the kid said, "So what did you think about the war between Hiroshima and Nagasaki?" It's hard for any of us to imagine life in a different time, and on top of that kids are trying to fit all the details in and sometimes they get confused about the specifics. Studying history means taking a lot of complicated experiences and compressing them. I was often astounded at how muddled the retelling could become. I think that when you teach from the textbook, it's also often muddled.

Most of my students came from middle schools where the textbooks were the curriculum. Instead, we used the text as a way of raising questions. I started collecting textbooks. I have a collection of 30 or 40 from the 50s to the present, each one different. When you look at them, I do believe that there was just one textbook that everybody copied, and just changed the sidebars and pictures. They're stultifyingly similar. The ones from the 60s are slightly more progressive and tip their hats to the civil rights movement and the women's movement with sidebars about people of color, women, and Native Americans.

Ellen: So what you're saying is that you're not ignoring the canon. You're having the kids learn the canon but encouraging them to question it.

Steve: Yes. However, by the 1990s, some things had shifted in the schools the kids were coming from. The canon didn't have the same impact. By the time the kids got to me they knew that Columbus wasn't such a good guy. At Coalition School for Social Change, I extended a unit we had developed at Bronx Regional. First we looked at Columbus's diary. It's excerpted in Howard Zinn's *People's History of the United States.* We looked at Columbus's words, and also the words of Bartolomé de las Casas, a priest who was among the first to ask for the end of the enslavement of the Taínos in Puerto Rico. De las Casas made this demand because of the way the Taínos were being treated. They were literally being worked to death. It tells us something about the attitudes in European society at that moment. And then we would look at contemporary textbooks. Every kid got her or his own textbook, different textbooks. There was no mention of Columbus's journal whatsoever. It raised all sorts of issues. If we know that there's a journal by Columbus and it's readily available, why is there no mention? Kids wrote letters to the publishers. It allowed them to take the information we had worked on in class and say, "Based on my understanding, and citing the sources, this is the way I understand what happened. How come it's not in your textbook?"

Ellen: Did they get answers?

Steve: One or two. They were almost form letters. I don't think we ever received a substantive answer.

Ellen: This is connected to point of view, which the students were working on with the interviews.

Steve: That's right. It raises questions about how history has been reported. And we can challenge it. We have access to other sources. We're not going to become historians necessarily, but we're not going to believe everything we read. It seems to me that politically our country is back to a place where we're circling the wagons, telling the traditional story again. That story dovetails conveniently with what's on the test. The two are the same, very close. This raises the question of point of view and ideology, which becomes crucial around issues of test prep. It's also an opportunity to look at things like the canon. Kids can know the story, and accept or reject pieces of it, but know that in this society it's the point of reference for most people. And the students can know the official story well enough to know why they agree or disagree.

Ellen: Say more about the link between the understanding you are helping kids develop and test prep.

Steve: Comparing primary sources with the text allows us to talk about how ideology changes the way we see history. I can say, "If you read the textbook, what's the point of view?" It takes discussion and some more examples. But it boils down to something like this: "This is a wonderful country. We've had problems in the past. If you look at the beginnings of our history there was slavery. Women couldn't vote. Only people with property could vote. But if you look at us now, despite our problems, there's been an enlargement of democracy. People can be in labor unions, women can vote, Black people don't have to sit in the back of the bus, and so on." So that big picture becomes the context for the test—which means that in most cases if you don't know the answer, if you remember that, you can probably choose the right answer.

Ellen: Because instead of cramming their memories full of discrete "facts," they learned how to analyze the test?

Steve: Right. Kids bring up questions and there needs to be time for that, even though it's test prep. It allows them to make connections to things we'd done before. Because I don't do test prep until the end of the year or semester, kids would say, "I remember when we talked about this in a different way." They were able to know the canon and measure it against an alternative way of looking at that history, or make new connections, or have new understandings. It was like being immersed in something, and hearing something, and thinking about it, and then hearing it again in a different context, and saying, "Now I understand it in a different way because of the new information I had. So it was important to allow enough time so you're not just prepping for the test.

There's a parallel. History is written as a construct. So are the tests. We can master that construct. We don't have to agree with it, but we can figure it out as a class, which we did. We went over past tests and picked them apart. So when kids walk into the test and think, "How am I going to do this?" they've seen something like it. The test is so similar from year to year that if you go over enough of the tests from previous years, you can figure it out.

I was able to take that information and prepare a study guide. I did that in the late 80s and kids are still using it because the tests are the same except for the current events section. I tell them that for the current events section there's a website where you actually can see each test with the answers, so the kids can update.

Ellen: Many people use previous tests to help kids prepare, but what's different about what you do is what comes before, and the perspective. Before the kids start the test prep they're able to go into something in depth and get a sense of what a historian would do.

Steve: Yes. Even though we focus on test prep for a period of time, it becomes an extension of what we've done all along, but in a different way. If you only do test prep and only use the textbook, that's what history becomes. But if you do it at the end of some real historical thinking and studying, it becomes a piece of that, but clearly distinct. We're saying, "This isn't history. This is a view of history you're being tested on."

Once we have some common understandings—we're products of a historical era, we're in it, affected by it—kids are interested in who they are and how they got to be that way. It's important to know our histories because we're part of the larger society. And it's important because we're connected to each other. Teaching anything gives people the opportunity—the students and the teacher—to figure out who we are. I always say to kids, "There are 23 of us in this room. It's sort of random. As a result of your history, your parents', where they met, my history, we all wind up in this particular place at this particular time. It's fascinating." That's interesting to me and interests kids, because they always want to talk about themselves. I always try to make room for that—what it raises, what it reminds you of, how our particular histories are connected to larger histories.

Ellen: I often hear teachers, especially of high school students, talk about how the kids are so disaffected, not interested in the curriculum. It sounds like you have a different starting point: They can be engaged.

Steve: They can be disaffected but, of course, it's not universal. I want to engage, and they know it. It goes back to the issue of viewpoint and multiple perspectives and creating opportunities so students can realize they have opinions and points of view that are valued in the class. I had a viewpoint, clearly. I didn't hide that. But I needed to create an atmosphere where I was just one voice among many.

Teachers say, "I'm supposed to be objective," but no one's objective. Then they wind up teaching stuff that has a particular point of view and they don't even know it because by calling it "neutral" or "objective" they accept it. So part of my teaching approach involves creating an atmosphere where we're really challenging ourselves and where everyone has a point of view that comes from some place.

My thinking about test prep included helping students develop an attitude: "We're going to show these people!" and "Working together, helping each other, nurturing each other will really get us through."

There was one kid when I was prepping kids for the Regents at the School for the Physical City. When we started talking about the test, he began to cry. He felt it was a personal affront to him on a number of levels but mainly because he wasn't expected to pass. "How dare they give me a test that they don't think I'm going to pass?" And he started to cry, this tall guy, in front of the class. And we all assured him that he would pass.

Ellen: "We all" meaning the other students?

Steve: Yes. And he passed. He felt he could do it. If I didn't have to give the test I wouldn't, because it pigeonholes people. It pigeonholes the teacher who feels pressured to get kids to pass and of course it pigeonholes the kids.

These were kids who had seen themselves as poor students. Some of them had taken the test a number of times and were convinced they couldn't pass and they couldn't learn history. They passed, and they learned something about themselves. It's powerful enough to do well at something you never thought you could do. But it had ramifications beyond the test. They'd walk away as people who said, "I can."

Kids say, "Teachers always want to know what I think, but they never tell me what they think." It becomes a guessing game. We all make assumptions. I walk into a classroom. I'm old. I'm odd looking. I'm white-skinned. Kids often say, "You live in the suburbs, right?" I had a picture of me sitting on a chair in Bennington College, on the campus. They would say, "That's your house. You live there, right?" I'd say, "Yeah, right. I've been living in Washington Heights since 1971." The kids would be shocked. "You live in Washington Heights??? You come from a rich family, right?" "No. I came from a poor family."

To me, part of teaching is creating a community, which allows all of us to come to know and respect each other. So I think teachers need to challenge the idea that because we look different, we must be vastly different. There are differences no doubt, because of age, class, and race. But the classroom can be a place where we can be open. You can't say, "We're going to look at history, but some questions are taboo." I would tell students, "What is taboo is being disrespectful to others. You can say anything you want here, but it needs to be done respectfully. People should feel free to disagree, not for the purpose of disagreeing but so you can really say what's on your mind and work it out." When kids start talking, you can actually hear them thinking. And if someone gets impatient, I'd have to say, "No. They're working it out." There's the space for it. The situation demands it.

PART II

In the Company of Teachers

Prospect's Descriptive
Review of Practice

While the classroom stories in Part I set the stage for the kind of education that nurtures possibility, the spotlight in this book is on the Descriptive Review of Practice. In the 1990s, Patricia Carini, in conversation with teachers in Mamaroneck and Phoenix, developed several processes that focus on the art of teaching. Carini characterizes the aim of these processes as creating "a vehicle for teachers to talk with each other about what actually happens in the classroom that involves the children in active pursuit of questions, issues, and interests of significance to them and leads to understandings which the teacher believes are educationally important" (Himley, 2011, p. 49). These processes bring together resources of story, observation, description, reflection, and documentation in a focused way. They establish a starting point for examination of classroom activity and curriculum. This is a different starting point from that established by practices such as aligning curriculum to state and national standards or "curriculum mapping."

In the Descriptive Review of Practice, it is the teacher's work that is central. Prior to the Review, the presenting teacher and chair meet to plan the session, and out of that planning the teacher decides what materials to bring, what aspects of the practice to include in his or her portrayal, and what the focusing question will be. Participants in the Review respond to that question only after hearing the teacher's full description and asking questions to pull forward more description.

The work of teaching overflows with activity. Reflection, which entails standing back from the immediacy of the classroom, is essential to a teacher's growth and satisfaction. A Review of Practice affords a teacher the opportunity to take both a wide-angle and zoomed-in view of his or her practice. The aim is not to be conclusive or exhaustive—an impossibility in any case—but to allow the teacher to describe what matters in teaching and to explore his or her own values as they play out within the ever-changing course of a teaching day and a teaching life.

In this section, two teachers present their experiences with Reviews of Practice, one with a transcript of an actual Review of Practice and the other with a description of the planning process leading up to a Review. These companion pieces provide windows on both a Review-in-process and the thinking, conversation, and planning that precede a Review.

In "Remembering the Child, Resisting Distraction" we meet Peg Howes, a 3rd-grade teacher, as she conducts a Review that explores places where her own values—what makes her feel she is "doing something good"—clash with the expectations of her setting. In this inquiry into her teaching practice she asks herself some hard questions: How is it that I can lose my bearings? Am I taking all the freedom I have? Do I let myself get seduced by the latest new thing? In grappling with her own situation, Peg invites us to think productively about the value conflicts that are a daily reality for so many teachers and to find possibilities for action.

In the second piece, "Round Tables and Grids," Bruce Turnquist describes the steps of preparing for a Review, working with a chair to clarify his goals and plan his presentation. Troubled when he finds himself out of step with new procedures in his school, he recounts the aspects of his situation that lead to his desire to do a Review of Practice. This time the focus is on the planning process, and we leave him as he anticipates his Review.

CHAPTER 6

Remembering the Child, Resisting Distraction

Peg Howes

[*Editors' note:* This chapter presents a Descriptive Review of Practice, one of Prospect's collaborative inquiry processes. The presenting teacher was Peg Howes and the chair was Ellen Schwartz. Most of the chapter is drawn from the transcript of the Review, but there are places where the chair addresses the reader directly. The aim of these comments is to make her thinking transparent. The chair's remarks to the reader are set in italics to indicate that they were not part of the Review itself.]

Two years ago a child came into my teaching life and launched me on a journey of inquiry that is reshaping my teaching. Sam was quiet at the start of his 3rd-grade year and slow to reengage with school routines after summer vacation. He didn't always remember to do his homework or bring back forms. But he was engaged with the curriculum. His contributions, especially in class discussions, revealed a person who thought deeply and reached to express complicated ideas. When my coteacher and I assigned a desert-animals project, Sam was captivated by the horned toad. He poured his heart into gathering information and making a poster. The children's finished products were to be graded by a rubric. When I looked at his poster, it was so confusing that I knew that by the standards of the rubric Sam would fail. I didn't let that happen. I couldn't let it happen because there was so much more to Sam's learning about the horned toad than the rubric could measure. What Sam did was jar my senses enough for me to realize that using rubrics to grade writing had distracted me from what was really important.

Making Space for Active Learning, edited by Anne C. Martin & Ellen Schwartz. Copyright © 2014 by Teachers College, Columbia University. All rights reserved. Prior to photocopying items for classroom use, please contact the Copyright Clearance Center, Customer Service, 222 Rosewood Dr., Danvers, MA 01923, USA, tel. (978) 750-8400, www.copyright.com.

51

This experience set me on a course. I told the story to a teacher friend and then I wrote about Sam and my use of rubrics. I wanted to explore how the grading rubric both narrowed my view of Sam and failed to support his own development as a writer. I brought what I had written to my educators' study group to do a close description of it. I asked: What did my story suggest to them? What did it let us think about? What questions did it raise? What might I want to look at in my teaching practice to examine these questions further? Subsequently, the study group spent a second session describing a story and picture made by Sam and looking at the rubric and Sam's story side by side. The description of his work brought Sam to life as a thinker and writer who elegantly incorporated his knowledge into what he wrote. The view of Sam's learning and depth of his involvement that emerged from our description sharply contrasted with what the rubric made visible.

These two study group sessions enlarged the scope of my inquiry. My questions were no longer just about Sam or rubrics. My simple classroom story had become a journey, an extended inquiry into my struggle to keep children in my sights. A Review of Practice seemed like a useful next step.

CHAIR'S INTRODUCTION

A Descriptive Review of Practice doesn't just happen. The process began when Peg and I met to plan the session. At this meeting Peg talked about the issues that were leading her to do a Review of Practice, and over the course of the meeting Peg formulated the questions that would provide a focus for the response of colleagues who would compose the study circle. In the planning, it was clear that this Review would provide an arena for Peg to explore the values in which her teaching was rooted, values that were increasingly at odds with practices in her school. A teacher's practice is infinitely complex, so Peg would have to decide which aspects of her practice to focus on. Peg and I talked through how she would describe her practice, including the headings that would provide a structure for the Review.

A Review always begins with contextual information about the setting and the teacher's relationship with it. This material would be presented under the heading "The Place." Following that, Peg would describe her practice under two headings: "What Matters to Me" and "What Gets in My Way." We felt that these headings would encompass the scope of Peg's practice and bring into relief the tension she was experiencing.

On the day of the Review, the participants gathered in a circle, notebooks in hand. The people who joined in to this Review, in addition to Peg and me, were Patricia Carini, Margaret Himley, Rhoda Kanevsky, Anne Martin, Gina Ritscher, Lynne Strieb, Bruce Turnquist, and Betsy Wice. As reader, you are entering the Review as I open the session.

OPENING THE REVIEW

Since we all know each other, I'll dispense with introductions and launch into the plan for today's session. I will briefly present a bit of Peg's history as a teacher and Peg's focusing questions for this Review. After that, Peg will go right into her Review. She will speak without interruption, so make notes of thoughts or questions that come to you along the way. After Peg's presentation, I will do an integrative restatement, and then open the session for clarifying questions. We'll end with responses to Peg's focusing questions— which will get restated later on—and with a round of comments to process.

Peg attended Prospect's teacher education program, graduating in 1984. She has worked as an elementary teacher in public schools in Vermont and New York, and for the last 11 years she's been at her present school, first as the enrichment teacher and subsequently as a classroom teacher, mainly in inclusion rooms. She currently teaches 3rd grade.

Peg's focusing questions for this Review are:

- In an educational atmosphere rife with distractions that claim Peg's time and pull her away from her core values, how can she hold onto these values and enact them in her teaching? How can she sustain a place for herself and her own practice and be a genuine participant in the school community?
- In Peg's school, curriculum and evaluation are driven by external standards about "what children should know," not by knowledge of individual children. In this context, how can Peg carve out as much space as possible for the children and herself to find depth and meaning in what they are doing together?

DESCRIPTION OF PRACTICE

The Place

My school is not a bad place to work. The town it serves is in many ways a typical upstate New York small town, but at the same time big changes are coming. It was a rural farming and small manufacturing community that is turning into a bedroom community for the urban area to the south. This change may speed up soon, because a large corporation is being courted to establish its corporate headquarters nearby. If that happens, much development will follow. Some forecasts estimate my school will double in enrollment.

My colleagues are a group in the midst of change. When I arrived, I joined a faculty made up primarily of local women who had grown up in the profession together and developed close bonds. As members of this group retire, they are being replaced by new teachers who grew up here or nearby. The senior teachers are powerful, strong-willed, opinionated women, who earned their power by enduring. They have worked hard, invested in the school community, and been influential. I respect them, but I don't always agree with them. Their influence is diminishing as their numbers decrease, but for now they are still a significant presence.

We've had a recent change in administrators, including my building principal of 9 years and the special education director. I'm sorry to see my principal go. We had a good working relationship. Conversation was easy and open ended with her.

The resources in my school are abundant. This stunned me when I arrived. I was coming from a tiny Vermont school with a decaying prefab school building, a dinky library that doubled as the computer lab, and a swampy playground. In contrast this school is well kept and immaculately clean with carefully maintained grounds. The interior is organized in grade-level quads with four to five classrooms at each level. The layout is very appealing to the first-time observer, but the architecture keeps us isolated in our own grade levels.

The campus includes a cafeteria, a gym, a beautiful library with a vaulted ceiling, two science labs, a state-of-the-art computer lab, abundant dry playing fields, and two playgrounds. Music, band, art, speech, occupational and physical therapy, Reading Recovery, academic intervention services, the school psychologist, and the school guidance counselor all have their own spaces. By next fall most classrooms will be outfitted with SMART Boards.

The Special Education Department has a suite of offices in my building. We have easy access to the special education director. Just drop in! The office staff is friendly, and they always have coffee. The cornerstone of the school's special education services is the inclusion classroom. There are inclusion rooms at every grade level, staffed by a regular education teacher and a special education teacher working as a collaborative team.

What Matters to Me: Expressing Myself in Teaching

I want to start talking about my practice with stories that show where it has been possible for me to express my values.

Inclusion Rooms. I was hired as the enrichment teacher for K–8th grade. When I chose to move to classroom teaching, my principal decided I would be a good bet for the inclusion rooms, and I embraced the idea from the start. I have been an inclusion room teacher for 7 years, first in 4th grade, now in 3rd. It is one place where I feel I have been able to be true to myself as a teacher.

I may as well say right off, what matters to me most are the children, my own classroom, and the curriculum. I want my students to see each other for who they are, not through labels such as special needs, gifted, low, average, or high. I believe this can be done with adequate support and have found the inclusion rooms to be a setting in which it is possible for children with a range of skills, knowledge, and experience to thrive together in a community of mutual respect.

I have been lucky to have a number of compatible teaching partners who share the same vision for the classroom. We have a sense of companionship and mutual respect. We have given ourselves permission to step away from textbooks and worksheets to develop our own materials. We mix and match students, grouping or pairing depending on the activity. We do lots of project work, looking for a variety of ways for children to show their knowledge. We try to do whatever makes sense to support the individual children. My partners and I have worked to create a warm and open classroom atmosphere for the children and for each other. The atmosphere is generated in part through curriculum. I'll give you an example.

The official reading program has always included the use of a reading series. At first I pretended that I was using it, by picking and choosing from the reading anthology, while looking for ways to use other kinds of reading material that had more depth. I also developed literature units that were not rooted in the reading series, such as a folktale study we do each year. I fill the room with folktales and fairy tales, play story tapes and read stories aloud. We are awash in stories. We make simple charts of stories and use them for group retellings. Children read stories together and retell them to each other. We write original "folktales," including *pourquoi* stories, such as "How the Snake Lost Its Legs," or new versions of classics like Cinderella and Red Riding Hood. Groups of children create plays of favorite stories. Finally, we invite families to a festival at which the children perform their plays, and their stories and illustrations are displayed.

The folktales project is important to me because it embodies values I try to enact:

- depth and thoroughness
- taking time
- taking something and making it your own
- collaboration
- sharing

Parents also reflect my values back to me. One parent who came to the folktale show this spring told me, "I really appreciate the fact you have all the children participate in the plays, and it's not just the kids who are the best students who are out there performing." This mother was speaking not just about the folktales, but also about a performance we had done earlier in the spring.

Another mom asked if she could bring in activities or projects to do with the kids. We planned together before she came in. She was happy to do exactly what I wanted, but I also encouraged her to follow her own instincts because I could count on her to bring in a worthwhile activity. This spring she brought tadpoles. She arrived when I was reading *The Prince of the Pond*, by Donna Napoli. It's the Frog Prince from the point of view of the prince, who's just become a frog. I was reading it because I love the book, it's full of frog information, and it's a way to connect folktales and frogs. The parent made a point of telling me how much she appreciated the connection of one subject to another.

Shaping the curriculum to have scope and depth makes me feel that I am doing something good. And yet I don't always do what I think is right, which is of course something that I worry about. I wonder if I have taken advantage of all the freedom I actually have.

Colleagues and the School Community. Beyond the satisfactions of the classroom and connections with parents, the opportunities I've had for contributing to the school as a whole widen the scope of my work and connect me. At present I'm a grade-level coordinator. As such I serve as a member of the Principal's Advisory Team, attending monthly meetings at which we discuss such items as the school calendar and schedule, the principal's initiatives, and issues and questions from the teachers. I also facilitate meetings of the 3rd grade and organize efforts to complete grade-level tasks, for example, curriculum work, making class lists for the next year, and planning field trips. I'm a conduit of information and directives between the 3rd grade and the principal. Sometimes this involves informing my colleagues about the latest mandates. My fellow teachers view the demands imposed on them by Washington and Albany, or by their own administrators, as the burdens of teaching. They complain about them, they argue, and then, out of a sense of duty, they do what they are expected to do.

For many years I was a member of the Child Study Team, to which teachers bring their concerns about students. I really liked my role because it gave me a chance to listen to what was going on with teachers at other grade levels and to offer support. I was also a member of the Science Curriculum Committee, which revamped our science program, and the Literacy Program Committee, which just spent a year examining our English/Language Arts program. I've been a new-teacher mentor for 7 years and served on the committee that wrote the mentoring plan. I've also sat on various hiring committees.

Coteaching is the place where I experience the greatest bond with colleagues. In our ongoing conversations, I get to think about children, classrooms, and teaching in a deeper and more intellectually satisfying way than in any other school context, except perhaps for parent conferences. One year the special education director formalized this kind of conversation by scheduling monthly meetings for inclusion teams to get together and share experiences. We brought stories of children and provided support for each other. They were good discussions with some depth of thought about children. With time and the addition of some structure, we could have become an even more effective study group for each other. Alas, this happened for a year, then stopped.

Though I have had opportunities to express my opinion on matters that affect us all, to influence decisions about children and to support teachers, I have to be cautious. To navigate the political realm at school, I listen for the openings where I can be most effective—small windows where I can insert a comment or raise a question. In trying to pick battles I know I can win, I wonder if I keep my mouth shut more than I should. Sometimes decisions get made that I don't like, despite my efforts to keep us talking and thinking. We have a tendency to move quickly to decisions. I wish we could spend more time thinking things through before we go into action.

This past year, after 7 years as an inclusion teacher, I had a class to myself. I needed a year alone to think about my own teaching without at the same time working at making space for somebody else's ideas and style. It was a good decision and a very good year. I discovered that I could be on my own and survive, more than survive—I could flourish. Next year I'll be back in inclusion, working with a new young teacher whom I mentored last year. Luckily, our ideas about inclusion match pretty well. Early last year she asked me if I thought it would be a good idea for her to keep journals on each of her students. I thought, "If she wants to write about her children, we'll definitely have things to talk about." And we did.

What Gets in My Way: The Distractions of School

I've been describing a teaching situation that has many positive attributes and some flexibility. "So," you might ask, "What's the problem?"

Well, I get distracted from the source of inspiration and authenticity in my teaching—the children. I want to cultivate a richly detailed knowledge of the children through watching them, seeing their work, and hearing their ideas. This perspective—of looking, absorbing the detail, and finding value there—is at the heart of my teaching, but it's a struggle to be thorough and thoughtful all the time, to keep my focus on what I learn from children. Teaching is exhausting and incredibly time consuming. You can work at it all the time, and still there is something else to do. So, I give in to what's easy, what's expected, what's glitzy—the latest new thing—even when I know better. I'm going to talk next about some of the things that distract me.

The Pace of the Day. From the moment I arrive in the morning I am in constant motion, barely stopping to catch my breath.

7:30: Leave home with a piece of toast and cup of coffee in hand (I plan to eat my yogurt as soon as I get to school, but never do.)

8:00: Arrive at school, get ready for the day (organize materials, look through completed assignments, put work on bulletin boards, organize books in library, assign classroom job on Monday, prepare weekly newsletter on Friday, prep for a sub if I have a meeting to attend).

9:00: Greet kids as they dribble in. Take time to say hello, ask a question, listen to a story, get someone to help pass out papers to go home or morning work materials. Soon more children arrive. Now I'm giving directions and responding to questions. Then, time for morning news if I've remembered to turn on the television.

9:20: Start Morning Meeting. Date, calendar, news, weather. Sharing follows. It's what the children have been waiting for. I'm watching the clock thinking we should get on to other things. I don't relax during sharing, which is too bad. Instead I'm anticipating 10:35, when Mrs. D. will take students for academic support. I want to get enough done before she gets here so whoever leaves has gotten a good start on work and will be able to pick it up again when he or she returns.

9:45: Begin English language arts. We start with a spelling or English lesson or go straight into reading followed by writing. Time slows down during reading. We think and talk about books, or the children work with each other on a project. The pace picks up again at 10:35 when Mrs. D. arrives and some children leave.

11:00: Have snack and story. Children wander, eat, and get boisterous, until I say, "OK, I'm going to read," and bring out the read-aloud of the moment. They listen, comment, ask questions, eat.

11:20: Go to specials. We are frequently late, because I always think I can stretch the time a little further. The specials teachers are gracious about this. They say, "As long as you pick 'em up on time . . . " Now I have time to regroup. I pick up my mail and talk to people I pass in the hall as I hurry back to the room to check homework and take a quick look at the next math lesson. I find out who has handed in homework and who didn't understand the math. I make my list of who will stay in for part of recess to complete homework and get extra help. Recess lasts only 15 minutes, so I feel bad when I keep children in, but there is no other time to catch them up.

12:00: Pick the kids up; start math. There's never enough time so sometimes I start math right after snack and pick it up again after specials, but only if snack doesn't take long and we don't have read-aloud. At the end of math, the children are anticipating recess and lunch, while I'm trying to introduce the homework assignment. Inevitably, I must accept that we've run out of time and save the rest for the afternoon.

12:40: Have recess and lunch. My homework group stays with me. At 12:55, I send them to lunch and head to the Staff Commons to eat. Or, I stay in the classroom to get materials ready for science and social studies. If I go to Staff Commons I get to spend time with my 3rd-grade colleagues. We talk about someone's upcoming marriage, the recent death of a colleague's husband, issues and questions people want me to bring to the Principal's Advisory Team meeting. At lunch I often discover that—in spite of my best efforts—I've forgotten to attend to some schoolwide matter, such as handing in a form, contributing to a baby shower collection, or signing up to bring food for a staff breakfast. I *never* reveal that I've forgotten; I just take care of the oversight as soon as I can.

1:15: Pick up the children; read aloud or finish math while they use the bathroom, a couple of kids at a time.

1:30: Begin science. The science program involves observing, lab procedures, record keeping, and discussion. The children are always interested. They work hard—thinking, talking to each other, looking, working with materials. I try to observe and listen to them, but I don't do enough, because I'm always checking the clock, anticipating what the program would have me do next.

2:30: Begin social studies. I hate this time of day, because I hate the textbook. I don't mind when I run out of time and can't do much. Generally, I don't feel I have planned adequately. But if I consider the studies I have developed—such as mapping, slavery and the Underground Railroad, country studies, and pioneer life—I see that I do more social studies than I think. Sometimes these studies start with the textbook as a jumping-off point, often not. Usually, they are focused on chapter books and movies, with more depth than our textbook. We often do these studies as reading, so I don't think of them as social studies.

3:00: Practice cursive. Quiet, calm, brief.

3:15: Start dismissal. Madness! A voice comes on the loudspeaker dismissing students whose parents pick them up. The first wave of buses departs around 3:25; more buses 5 minutes later; last bus at 3:40. While we wait, students do homework, read, or play a game. It's a long time at the end of a long day.

3:40: Organize my desk, clear off the big work table, get out materials for the next day, gather up work to review and grade, pack my bag, and head home. I generally don't get out before 4:30, sometimes later.

The Latest New Thing. Along with the rapid-fire pace of the day, I feel besieged by the onslaught of one new thing after another. In my school there is a push to buy the latest programs and equipment, without thinking through all the implications—both positive and negative—for the classroom. An example is the decision this spring to purchase a new reading series. Our literacy committee had begun to identify areas needing improvement. These were fruitful conversations. I was especially interested in the work of a 1st-grade teacher. She was trying to make major changes—getting away from phonics workbooks and an unsatisfactory reading series. She was scrambling to find or make enough copies of reading materials she wanted to use. Though challenging, the changes she made were valuable and felt right. Other 1st-grade teachers were also making changes and supporting each other. I was impressed. Then . . .

Suddenly this spring we were looking at several new reading series. The impetus for this came from the 1st-grade teachers, including the one who had been working so hard to change her practice. Anticipating the imminent departure of our principal, they wanted something new in place to use in September, because they didn't want to go through another year with insufficient, inadequate reading materials. And logic dictated that the school couldn't just purchase a reading series for 1st grade. We needed to buy something for everybody.

And *then*, we bought one at the cost of $100,000. And what was the lure? Our new reading series appears to have everything: online access; integrated vocabulary, spelling, grammar, and writing; leveled readers; cross-curricular connections; range of genre; abundant assessment; alignment with state standards—lots of bells and whistles.

I worry that having to learn this new system will be overwhelming. I worry the reading material will be shallow and the activities will be mediocre, but I'll still have to use them. I worry that it will consume my time and distract me from what I think is important.

I have the same worries about SMART Boards. My district initiated a plan to increase our use of technology. For next year this means SMART Boards in most classrooms and websites for everyone. SMART Boards are very appealing to the children, who learn to use them with ease, and I am not immune to the attraction. I will learn to use mine, but I know that this, too, will take time away from doing a better job at other things that are important to me. Designing and building a new website is another time-consuming distractor. Once some of my colleagues have their websites up and running, I will feel the pressure to conform.

Other teachers seem to embrace all this new stuff without question, and become masters of it. I question these innovations. Am I just whining about making changes? Have I become "old school"? My colleagues seem competent and confident about their own teaching practice. In contrast, I wonder if I am doing enough. Am I covering all the bases? Will my students fail to progress, and will I be uncovered as a fraud, not a real teacher? Distract me enough, I lose my grounding and my self-confidence too.

Grading and Rubrics. Grading is another requirement of the job that pulls my focus away from the children. It distracts me from what I consider good curriculum because assignments need to be gradable. I do what I have to do to generate the report card.

Sometimes I assign work just to get a grade, as for English grammar. Though I believe students learn about grammar most effectively through writing, talking, and reading, my English grades are based on exercises from the textbook. When the children work on writing pieces, there are other opportunities to address grammar and do more meaningful teaching of issues related to language structure, usage, and word choice, all in the service of expressing ideas. So I don't feel that my superficial treatment of grammar through the use of the textbook is so bad, but still I feel that I'm taking the easy way out.

Spelling assignments fall into the same category—work given to get a grade. In the past, I have been obsessive about "the right way" to set up an assignment in the spelling notebook. When I worry about something like format, it's because I'm thinking about the children going to 4th grade, where some teachers may be more concerned with such issues. But why should I worry about this? I'm feeling pressure, perhaps self-imposed, about the expectations at the next grade level.

I am most uncomfortable grading written work and projects. They seem more important because they are so clearly expressive of the child, unlike, for example, a fill-in-the-blank worksheet. I want to be respectful of the child's effort to produce a piece of work that shows his or her thinking, without comparing it to abstract standards or to the work of other children. But I have to grade this expressive work, and my grading process has become routine. I do what is easy, efficient, and expedient. After a while a person gets numb, and routines become unexamined practice. That's how I got sucked into using rubrics.

Sam

This leads me to Sam's story. Sam was a student of mine and became the impetus for doing this Review of Practice. The story begins 2 years ago. I had a new teaching partner who was young, energetic, and quite new to teaching. Early on we discussed grading. Our goal was to be honest, accurate, and fair. We talked about making the grading criteria clear to the children from the start. My partner was eager to try rubrics to score the children's written work, so we decided to design a rubric for the final projects in a desert study. The children were asked to research a desert animal and were given a choice of either writing a report or making a poster with drawings and captions to convey the information they had learned. We designed a rubric to score each choice.

We introduced the project choices using the rubrics, so the children knew from the start what the requirements were. We also showed the children my partner's sample poster and her report on the spade-foot toad to demonstrate finished product examples. We even had the children score her work using the rubrics. The kids responded enthusiastically.

Sam was a child whose stories were as much drawn as written. The drawn parts contained a significant amount of information, so I was not surprised when he went for the poster. He picked the horned toad because it can shoot red goo out of its eyes to scare away predators. Sam thought that was very cool and was highly motivated to find out more. He was independent while browsing through books to gather information on his topic and while making his poster. On the last day the children had for their projects, I had a chance to look at Sam's work.

What I saw was fascinating—and scary. It was one of those kinds of drawings that are hard to "read" because the point of view isn't immediately evident. It seemed as though Sam had started in the middle of the page and spiraled out to the edges, along the way drawing and captioning little scenarios for the toad. Adding to the challenge of interpreting the poster was Sam's handwriting, which was always difficult to read, but was made more so by his arrangement of space and use of speech bubbles. He had made tiny bubbles, then tried to write in them. It just didn't work.

I could see that Sam had poured his heart into learning about the toad and making his poster, and I knew that, judged by our rubric, it would not fare well. The rubric would prevent us from giving credit for Sam's knowledge and effort, because the poster needed Sam to act as interpreter. I felt responsible for setting Sam up to fail.

That experience raised red flags for me. Even as common sense was telling me that rubrics were no cure for my ambivalence about grading, their allure had caught me. Rubrics seemed to offer an appealing discipline—plan and outline your grading standards, make them clear to the students—that felt purposeful, logical. Lucky for me I had a student like Sam, because he brought a lot of issues to the surface, beginning with the limitations of rubrics.

Like any system, a rubric is designed to let you look at certain aspects of a child's work, and is blind to everything else. Our rubric required 10 facts about the animal. It asked for a title, accurate spelling, creativity, neatness, and effort. Sam wasn't paying attention to proving what he had learned about his animal or the level of "finish" he achieved in his product. He was just engaged with the animal and with making a representation of it. He was very pleased with what he had produced. Not until he had to show his work to me did we realize it was hard to understand. Sam and I worked on trying to make it more understandable. As for grading him, in the end I ignored the rubric and gave him a grade that acknowledged how much work he'd put into his poster and how much he knew. By placing the emphasis on his product, the rubric masked his strengths: the way he immerses himself in a project, the scope of his thinking, his knowledge of the subject matter, and his confidence.

I was wrestling with contradictory thoughts. Sam was not working up to the standard I had set. And yet he had clearly learned a lot. Sometimes I just have to remind myself to have faith in children. No, he was not putting in the periods or capital letters, and his spelling was incorrect now, but eventually that would become important to him. At the same time, I worried about holding my students to a reasonable standard for finished products, and wondered about what the next grade level would expect.

My experience with Sam reminded me that the product is not the child. There was so much more to Sam's learning about the horned toad than the rubric could measure. Sam jarred my senses enough for me to realize that using rubrics to grade writing had distracted me from what was really important—how to help children learn to write. That's where I want to place more of my attention.

THE REVIEW CONTINUES

As chair, I was making notes as I listened to Peg's descriptions. I was alerted by Peg's headings to listen for tensions around value, which I pulled forward in my integrative restatement. This is a sort of summary, but the point was not simply to restate what I had just heard. Rather, it was to pull forward the connections and contrasts I was noticing, as a first pass through the wealth of material Peg had shared. What follows is an excerpt that captures the large themes of Peg's description.

Chair's Integrative Restatement

What Peg values most in teaching is the opportunity to get to know each child and to create a classroom community wherein each child's uniqueness is recognized by both adults and children. It is important to her that her teaching choices—including but not limited to curriculum—enable children with diverse needs and skills to flourish. This is why, for instance, she has all the children participate in the folktale plays, which was so appreciated by a parent. Peg sometimes tweaks and sometimes ignores the required curriculum in order to create these opportunities for children. Her folktale study is a prime example.

Peg also values genuineness. In her classroom children and parents can make contributions that express who they are. On the collegial level, Peg values relationships where there is a shared interest in understanding children, such as those with her teaching partners. She has many connections with colleagues—working closely with her teaching partners, mentoring new teachers, and serving on various committees. Peg sometimes feels she can be herself in these situations, but often she feels that she is holding back and in some ways feels isolated.

The many pressures on Peg's time and focus—such as curriculum mandates, grading requirements, and the relentless pace of the day—fragment her teaching life and interfere with her ability to enact her values as fully as she would like. Peg values the depth of exploration that large spans of time make possible, but she always feels rushed and tries to stretch time to suit her pace. She worries that the demands of her setting pull her away from those things that let her know she is "doing something good." She knows how easy it is to get seduced by practices that promise clarity, like rubrics. The jarring experience with Sam put Peg's value conflicts into sharp relief. Peg is aware that she does have some freedom of action and wonders if she is using all the freedom she has.

Clarifying Questions

The participants in the Review had been listening intently and making their own notes. After a short break, we entered the next phase, in which members of the group asked Peg questions designed to amplify and clarify her description of practice. As chair, I introduced this phase of the Review by stating that it was important to stay with questions and not slide into responses to Peg's focusing questions just yet. We were still gathering information about Peg's practice that would inform our responses.

Anne and Lynne led off the questioning.

Anne: I'm wondering what the make-up of this inclusion class is and how children get in there.

Peg: Most of the classes are not more than 25 kids. It varies from year to year, but as many as a third of the kids could have some sort of special ed labeling. Some have significant issues and others are more independent. When we figure out grade placements, we start by placing the special ed students in the inclusion room. As we assign other children to that room we take care not to overload the class with extremely needy children in addition to the kids with Individualized Education Programs (IEPs). We make a point of ensuring that the inclusion room is not a dumping ground. Some parents find out that their kids are in an inclusion class and worry about it. Those parents often seek us out right away and we talk about the fact that the room will not feel different for their kids. It'll work just fine.

Lynne: The school must be making Adequate Yearly Progress. Is that why you still feel you have some freedom in your curriculum?

Peg: Yes. The children tend to perform well on state tests. That has kept us safe from those highly scripted programs that other "less successful" schools have been forced to use.

As the discussion developed, collegial relationships became a focal point. People sought to understand more fully how Peg's relationships with colleagues affected both her involvement in her school and her sense of isolation. They were also exploring where the openings were for the sort of conversation that she finds sustaining.

Peg: In general, I feel that there's something missing for me in the quality of the dialogue in my school. What would satisfy me would be conversations that are grounded in children. As a grade level we have had occasional opportunities to talk about what we're doing in reading and writing. They're interesting conversations when they're focused on what people are actually doing with the kids. And we always say, "We should be sharing this stuff," and then we don't because there's no structure other than our shared planning time, which is already full.

Further questions about colleagues led Peg to delve more deeply into her feelings of isolation.

Pat: You mentioned colleagues—that the inclusion people have tended to be good partners and that some colleagues have been really helpful. I was also hearing about people leaving, including your supportive principal. I could picture all of these but I didn't get the feeling of collegiality in some fashion, and I didn't want to assume that without asking you.

Peg: I would say that the people with whom I have had really strong collegial relationships have either left the district or been moved to the other building. I've been thinking about who is left with whom I'll be able to talk about the things that matter to me.

Betsy: It seems that one of the things that makes you have a zest for coming to work is the collegial relationships. It's not like, "OK, I'll go it alone." Is that accurate?

Peg: Yes. It feels very lonely, and I feel burdened by not having people to talk to.

Pat: Another thing that you said—and they may both be true—is that you respect many of your colleagues, but when something new comes down on them they complain and then they cave and do whatever they're asked to do. Is that right?

Peg: Well, I would have to say that sometimes we are given tasks that we don't want to do, like aligning curriculum with state standards.

People grumbled about this because it felt like we were going over old ground: "Oh, we did this 10 years ago and we're doing it again." It's that kind of chatter, to get rid of anxiety about a task that seems confusing, tiresome, and maybe not even necessary. I have come to accept that as something that they do and then they do the work. It's not that they cave in . . . well, we *do* cave into things that we feel powerless to change.

In another exchange, Peg recounted comments she had made in a meeting about which reading series to choose.

Peg: A major concern I have about the reading series—based on my experience with the last one we bought—is that there might be reasonably good stories in the anthology, but the themes were always shallow and the questions and activities for children were a waste of time and confusing. It's important that what the kids are asked to do is worth doing.

Ellen: Do you think there'll be a space for people to keep talking about some of the issues you raised about the reading series? Or do you think that now that they've bought the series it's all going to become about implementation?

Peg: I think the Literacy Committee won't meet anymore, and the discussion at my grade-level meetings will turn to how do we implement it or how it isn't working. But I might be wrong about the Literacy Committee dissolving. It may be that some people will have to ensure that the people selling us this material provide the training they promised. I think the implementation will only be successful if there's training from the book company.

Betsy drew the questioning period to a close.

Betsy: Looking back on the year, are there things you would have liked to have more time to do in your classroom? If so, what?

Peg: I could have done a lot more with writing stories because the children loved it. I started doing that after all the tests were over, and they just took to it. If I had started that sooner, it would have been a good thing.

Integrative Restatement

At this point, as chair, I pulled together main themes, focusing my restatement on a tension that stood out to me.

Peg is engaged in so many ways in the school—with the children, with the families, on many committees, as the grade level liaison. At the same time she feels really isolated. It seems that the isolation has to do with not having colleagues with whom she can have conversation that's rooted in what she values. It's like she's always having to cross that bridge and speak something of their language in order to be in the conversation, in order not to feel alone. It's not surprising that she sometimes feels like a fraud, an imposter in an alien land.

Responses to Focusing Questions

I announced the transition to the next part of the Review by restating Peg's focusing questions and by reminding people that their responses could take the form of recommendations, but didn't have to. Peg would be listening and making notes and, later, sifting through these ideas as she continued to think about actions she could take.
      Margaret led off with a penetrating comment.

   Margaret: I was struck by what you described as a school that's so
      beautiful, so organized and efficient, so smooth running . . . and
      so unbelievably alienating. In some ways that's harder to disrupt
      than a school situation where children are under extreme pressure
      and the teacher has got to *do* something. At your school there's no
      urgency. There is nattering, and this false confidence because the
      scores are OK. Nothing touches that confidence, so the opening
      for discussion is hard to find. It's a really disturbing situation.
   Pat: What this is making me think about is the impenetrable culture of
      comfortable schools. That's an issue unto itself. It's not only about
      your particular situation.

   A number of people made suggestions that addressed Peg's desire to hold onto and enact her values, to sustain a place for herself in her school and to keep children at the center of her work.

   Rhoda: I wonder whether you could invite other 3rd-grade teachers
      to join in the folktale project, or perhaps a different project the
      whole 3rd grade could do together. It could be an opportunity for
      people to look at actual things kids do.
   Bruce: Even if you can't bring off something this ambitious, you might
      be able to join with one other teacher on a project, just some way
      to open up something with another colleague.
   Betsy: I'm thinking about the reading series. Maybe you and your
      colleagues could sit around with the anthology, ignoring the other

apparatus and the questions at the end of the unit. Just sit with
the anthology, flip through it and see what you all recognize. You
know: "Oh, I read a good kids' novel by that author." Have it be
a session that you have control of rather than the representatives
from the company.

Anne: I'm remembering what you said about wanting to do more story
writing and starting it earlier. That wouldn't take a lot of extra
time and you can combine it with other subjects. If you tell the
kids they won't be graded, they're going to just write and think
about what they're writing.

*Responding to the ideas people had shared, Margaret returned to the
issue of penetrating the façade of confidence.*

Margaret: I think these are all fabulous suggestions. They're about
starting small and starting from things that are already happening.
I was thinking that a context in which everyone is so confident
carries with it a lot of implicit competition. There's always that
sense of, "Oh my goodness, I don't know that I can do this." And
there's no space to share that. I'm wondering if the idea of small
failures could be a way to begin, if you do choose to initiate some
conversations. So Sam could be presented as a small failure that
led to a big idea. It could be another opening for people to talk
about anxiety and struggle besides carping and nattering and then
getting on with it.

Pat shifted the focus to Peg's constant feeling of being rushed.

Pat: Time is always being pushed to the edge. You're always trying to
stretch time to suit your pace. I was realizing that a lot of things
that have a natural mesh were being dealt with in small time
blocks. I wonder if there would be a way for you to preconceive
those parts of your teaching day over which you have control and
give yourself the benefit of bigger blocks of time.

It also felt to me that those many layers of minutiae
were draining your energy. There are zillions of tiny things
to attend to and nobody raising fundamental questions. If
the fundamental questions never come up, then the nattering
goes on. But if there are people who are willing to keep a
conversation going that's rooted in children and practice, that
would be a wonderful thing. Then you get back to the bigness
of what can happen with kids.

Comments to Process

A Review of Practice usually ends with comments to process. As chair, I introduced this.

> *Ellen:* We're going to shift gears now and talk about the process itself. What was your experience of participating in this Review? Were we respectful of Peg, her work, and each other? Do you have questions about any aspects of the session or decisions Peg made in preparing and presenting her practice?
>
> *Rhoda:* What was so helpful in this Review is that it contained descriptive material that is specific. Being specific is so important. One of the challenges of preparing a Descriptive Review of Practice, especially when you're new to it, is taking the time to gather all the specifics and not going general too quickly. The other thing is talking about the positives as well as the problems. Sometimes people use a heading that I've always loved: "What's Working and What's Not Working." As simple as that is, it's important to keep in mind, and you did.
>
> *Lynne:* This process differs from the Descriptive Review of the Child, because the headings accord with the focus of the teacher.
>
> *Ellen:* They evolve in response to the teacher's practice and questions.
>
> *Margaret:* But there *were* headings. It's an example of what can happen in a structured conversation versus a gripe session. It has so much to do with structure, which gives shape to the Review.
>
> *Betsy:* In a Review of Practice, you don't know what the headings will be until after you've worked through the planning. The headings Peg chose are not the only ones she could have selected. That, to me, connects with the idea of teaching as an art. Because each teacher's practice is a work in progress and needs to be described in its own terms, the Review of Practice does not start from a set protocol.
>
> *Rhoda:* I just looked back at the focusing questions. Within each of them is something about making space or sustaining one's place. There was a continuity and focus to what Peg said. I have the feeling that just articulating these questions became the first step toward addressing them.
>
> *Ellen:* And yet the story Peg told wasn't *determined by* her questions. Problem-solving protocols would begin, "So here's Peg's problem." Then the whole presentation would be focused on the problem and solutions. Hearing first about Peg's setting and about where she *can* enact her values gave the Review a very big canvas.

When we addressed the focusing questions I could think about them as more than problems to be solved.

Gina: We're addressing questions, but what we collect is not only about those questions. We're trying to collect material that will furnish a full and multidimensional picture of the practice, not to be strictly limited by the questions or the headings. That's what makes it phenomenological. It's very inviting because of that.

Peg: So you all are describing your experience of the process as full and multidimensional. As the presenter, coming in this afternoon I did not feel confident that I had covered all my bases. I was thinking, "Oh my God, there are all these other things I could say so much about!" But I trusted that the clarifying questions would pull out additional information.

Betsy: I found it striking that there was this oscillation between extreme confidence in what Peg knew and extreme self-doubt. This process makes room for both those things to happen. And it's not like they happen in succession—that you have all these doubts and they get resolved. It made it much easier to connect with it, because what Peg did *not* model was the "impenetrable culture of confidence." It was penetrable because of the depth. I think maybe that's at the root of this whole process. That someone comes to it in a kind of humility. Which makes lots of entry points for ideas, for people's input, and for a wide range of thinking.

AFTERTHOUGHTS

It's been a few years since my Review of Practice, and even more time has passed since Sam was my student. And yet these experiences stay with me. It interests me that a small classroom story like Sam's can be the start of something so much bigger. I talked about Sam launching me on a journey of inquiry. The image of a pebble dropped into a deep pond comes to mind. Sam was the pebble. The Review of Practice was one of the outer rings, but not the end. In fact there isn't an end to the concentric rings, or to my inquiry. It's fair to say that an effect of the Review of Practice was to remind me that wondering, inquiring, is a thing that I do.

Did I really forget what matters to me? No, but the cumulative effect of my environment with its values of simplicity, efficiency, and speed had obscured my vision. These values, at odds with my own, made me look away from what matters and spend too much time and energy spinning my wheels and worrying: "Is what I do enough? Am I on the right track? Could this next new thing be the silver bullet or a waste of time? Or am I a fraud, and will I be exposed?" Worries that are fruitless and exhausting. The Review of Practice gave me space and time to step back, to lay out the terrain of my work life, and to have a look at it with other thoughtful people. Doing the Review pulled to the fore my own obscured values. I could see them again: the importance of knowing the children as individuals, of creating a classroom community where their individuality is honored and valued by all, of making teaching choices that give everyone access and allow each of us to contribute in ways that express who we are.

A lasting effect of the Review is that remembering what matters to me helps keep me steady on my course. Do I go through a daily litany (I believe in . . .)? No, but moments arise when something jars me, and I notice. For example, in the year following the Review I had occasion to speak with my principal about a new requirement to give all reading program Unit Tests to all students regardless of their level of reading achievement. One of my students was working hard to develop as a reader but was not even close to the level at which she could read the test. I asked if it was really necessary to administer the Unit Tests to students who couldn't really read them. He responded by asserting that it was important for us to be consistent with these "benchmark assessments," which meant everyone must take the tests. I said, "So you are saying I should give this test, even though it will be an exercise in futility for her, because she can't read it." He knew the child, knew she would only get angry if made to take a test she couldn't do. He recognized how counterproductive it would be for her when she was working so hard to learn to read. He said, "Hmmm. I see your point." Knowing what really matters gives me the conviction to have a conversation like that. Am I always able to hold my ground? Not always, but I think I am not so easily overwhelmed now.

I understand with even more certainty that the right kind of conversation about children and teaching is fundamentally important to me. The disciplined conversation of my Descriptive Review of Practice—and the other related processes, such as Descriptive Review of the Child and Descriptive Review of Children's Work—satisfy this requirement. For this reason, I attend an inquiry group as often as I can. There is something about the descriptive processes that opens up time and space for the presenter and the other participants. As the presenter at my Review, there was space and time to tell a detailed story and to be genuinely heard and responded to. For the participants, there was space and time to listen to someone else's experiences and find places that resonated with their own. The commitment to close listening, to being patient, and the confidence that something of worth will occur creates this timeless and roomy environment. The layering of story and conversation and lots of time allows you to get to underlying values.

Compare this to the quality of conversation in many school-based discussions. There are superficial similarities. There is a person chairing or facilitating the meeting. There is a focus. Participants are expected to talk.

There the similarities end. At school, the more dominant personalities often rule the discussion. The goal is to say what you want to say, rather than to hear and respond to what everyone has to contribute. The outcome of the meeting is a solution to a problem, a list of tasks to be performed, in other words, a conclusion. The atmosphere of my Review of Practice was entirely different and much more satisfying because of its power to reveal what is worth thinking about.

I return again to Sam's small story, expanded to something bigger than itself, for this is another power of the Review process: to reveal how very complicated and fascinating is the business of being a person and the business of educating people. I relish the complexity, but I think this is not a view commonly held in schools, where the most evident values are, as I said, simplification, efficiency, and speed. There is nothing simple in teaching, no perfect reading program, and no rubric that will make grading easy. Perhaps the most fundamental lesson I take from my Review is that a *simple* teaching life is a mirage.

CHAPTER 7

Round Tables and Grids

Paving the Way to a Review of Practice

Bruce Turnquist

[*Editors' note:* This chapter, like Chapter 6, includes occasional comments by the chair of the Review. These are identified as Chair's Interludes and set in italics.]

The setting: a round table. A kindergarten and grade 1 teacher sit across from one another. The grade 1 teacher is taking notes, based upon the kindergarten teacher's information about children soon to be in this 1st-grade classroom. A few samples of work are present in the middle of the table . . . . As the teacher in grade one, I appreciate the opportunity to have conversations with our kindergarten teachers. Just getting together and attending to the children themselves is of great value. There is this sense of passing on the responsibility of teacher through sharing understanding about each child.

I have been teaching at Clow Community School in a small, rural New England town for 25 years. The school serves a student population of more than 500 students, a population that has doubled during my years there. I remember times when my own classroom practice and the values and practices of the larger school community have fit together, hand in glove. One period during which the fit was good occurred in the late 1980s through the middle of the 1990s, when our school became familiar with the work of the Prospect School and learned about the Prospect descriptive processes. As we practiced these processes, we came to realize that learning could not be separated from the learner. Knowledge of the individual child became central for many of us.

In recent years, I have become increasingly disquieted about my place in my school. After teaching in grades 2, 3, and 4 for most of my career, in the early 2000s I returned to grade 1, where I had started, and found signs of some disturbing changes. What I had taught as a grade 2 curriculum a dozen years before was now essentially the grade 1 curriculum. Kindergarten, too, had changed. Children were expected to begin learning to read in kindergarten, not just those children who were ready readers, but *all* children.

In addition, the process we used for placing children with their next teacher was changing. In the past, I would join my colleagues around a table and we would talk about the children in our classes. These conversations were necessarily descriptive because, in order to place the children, we felt the need to better know them. At these meetings we would make known which children received special education services, especially if these services included a classroom paraprofessional. While we recognized that some children would take more time and energy than others, we generally cross-checked this factor *after* making up our drafts of class lists.

Recently, school administrators had introduced a new process for placing children in the next grade. Classroom teachers were given a Student Needs Sheet, a cross-hatched grid on which we were to sort children as Individualized Education Program (IEP) Identified, Low Not Coded, 504 Students, Issue Children, and Need Additional Academic Challenges. For special education, "low," and 504 children, we were expected to indicate whether they were 1, 2, or 3 years behind grade level in each subject area, a total absurdity in the case of kindergarteners and 1st-graders.

As I sat in my classroom a few days before our placement meeting, considering where to place students on the grid, I became increasing uncomfortable. I was particularly stuck on Alice. She had been characterized as "slow" by some, but she had been quick enough to save our class play from my mistake when I had skipped a scene change. She had entered the performance from the audience and taken on her part without pause. I also remembered her wit, apparent in the drawing of a doghouse with her sister's name above the door. Alice did struggle with number work and sometimes seemed not to understand what I thought was a straightforward explanation, but one word or one box could not describe her.

DESCRIPTIVE REVIEW OF PRACTICE

The grid system for placement, which I found so inappropriate with regard to Alice, signaled the shifts that were so worrisome to me. I felt that what I cared most about as a teacher was becoming less valued within my school community. I was wondering how I might maintain, or even create, some space to speak differently and to keep what I valued central to my teaching. This prompted me to think about presenting a Descriptive Review of Practice.

Fortunately I would have the opportunity to do one at Prospect's Summer Institute on Descriptive Inquiry, in which I had participated for many years. This institute is a collaborative that gives us the chance to study children and our own teaching. I was preparing to be part of a 3-day spanning study. In fact, I would be the focus of this study as I described my teaching practice, ranging through my career at Clow Community School.

The chair for my Review, Ellen Schwartz, was also an elementary teacher, someone I knew through many years' participation in various Prospect activities. Throughout the spring and early summer, Ellen and I had corresponded by email and talked on the phone. Meanwhile, I was revisiting my own history as a teacher by making a thorough search through boxes, long sealed in my basement, unearthing works left behind by students years before and rereading my writings from over the years. Out of that dusty enterprise I had selected material that I thought would reveal some of the interests, ideas, and guiding principles that animated my teaching life.

CHAIR'S INTERLUDE ONE

When I arrived at Bruce's house for our planning meeting, Alice's work was out on a table. Our conversation began with informal talk about what was "up" for Bruce. He talked a lot about Alice and also some other children. Together we looked at Alice's work, describing informally to each other what we noticed. We also watched a short video of a class play, the one in which Alice had saved the scene, and a longer video of a reading share. All of this was giving me a feel for Bruce's classroom and his teaching, invaluable context for chairing his Review.

I always feel that the first step in chairing a Review of Practice is just becoming familiar with the teacher and his classroom. Children's work, material from class projects, and conversation with the teacher give me glimpses of his practice, and as we talk it is inevitable that the teacher's concerns—which eventually will be formulated as a focusing question for the Review—come out.

As we look together at material the teacher brings to the planning session, I have an eye out for things he might describe in the Review and things he might bring for the participants to see. This is something we'll discuss as the planning proceeds—a little suggestion here or there about what he might bring. There is so much going on in teaching, so one challenge of doing a Review is selection, deciding what to describe to the group so they will be able to respond to the teacher's focusing question.

Bruce was going to have the luxury of doing his Review as part of a spanning study, which means that there would be more opportunities than usual for people to describe material from his teaching life. But selection was still an issue. For instance, he had done massive amounts of writing and would have to narrow it to a manageable selection for the participants to read.

NOT GRIDDING ALICE

Early on in our planning meeting, I talked about Alice. I first heard about her at a September meeting to discuss the children who were about to enter my 1st grade. I was sitting around the table with Lois, her kindergarten teacher, and Fay, the special education teacher. Some of Alice's work was in front of us. "I just can't figure her out," Lois said. "She just doesn't seem to learn in the way that most other children learn." Fay suggested that we watch her closely: "She may be a candidate for special ed."

As it turned out, because of what I saw about Alice as a learner during her grade 1 year, I did not refer her to the special education system. I felt almost settled about this action. Still, I knew that another teacher might have done the opposite. Lois had it right. Alice was a puzzle. In a school system that values fixing problems through categorization, the mystery of Alice was likely to be "solved" through testing and checklists.

From past experience, I had come to see that a referral tended, ironically, to shut down questioning about a child or at least to channel it into prescribed formulae. The year before Alice was in my class, I had made a special education referral. During a meeting with the special education teacher, who would write the IEP, I expected to use material we had gathered on the student, my own reports and examples of student work, reports from school personnel, and information from a psychologist hired by the child's parents. This did not happen. I was asked a few questions, then told that this child sounded just like another student this teacher had. She would write the IEP easily, using many of the other student's goals. Instead of settling on a quick resolution of my own responsibility to Alice by turning her over to this system and way of thinking, I decided to hold open the questions, at least for a while.

I also talked with Ellen about the new placement process and the Student Needs Sheet. For the last couple of years, the focus of the placement meetings had gravitated to the impact of having children with IEPs in classrooms. There was a push to start with the children who had been the biggest "issues" in our classrooms, predistributing them before going through our regular process. Still, the actual gridding of children on the Student Needs Sheet disturbed me. Seeing this visual representation caused me to seriously question how we were coming to see children.

There were still unofficial opportunities for teachers to do Descriptive Reviews of Children, but they weren't part of the "official" view. Several of us were accustomed to taking a descriptive stance and genuinely valued it. It isn't that we had changed as people. What worried me was that by putting children into boxes, into those tidy categories, we might remold our ways of seeing. It seemed a little bit insidious, almost tempting. I thought, "The official view is easier to manage. We're so overloaded with record-keeping and having to justify our programs. With those pressures we just may be willing to take the easy way out." Gridding was not messy. Like with Alice. I could just designate her as "Low Not Coded" and leave it at that.

CHAIR'S INTERLUDE TWO

I could see that the changes at Bruce's school were monumental. They were made up of small acts, perhaps, like the introduction of the Student Needs Sheet, but at the heart of Bruce's concern was a shift in values. The school where he had worked for most of his teaching life, the school his own children had attended, was becoming a different place. I wanted to understand how these changes were affecting other aspects of Bruce's teaching life, so I asked him to tell me about that. He has chosen key stories from what he told me and organized them broadly under headings that capture the areas in which the changes were having worrisome effects.

GETTING TO KNOW EACH OTHER

I recalled an image from the first day of school. On that day, I set aside procedural matters such as the lunch count until we have established a working circle that includes us all. I ask children to recognize themselves in descriptions I give of them, such as, "This person's sister is starting grade 3 today. He was in Mrs. Paine's kindergarten class last year, and he is wearing a bright red shirt." Recognition dawns on the child and upon the faces of many of the other children. In this way we name ourselves together, making introductions and identification specific to the person.

Next, those who are ready to do so share how they are feeling about the first day of school. I start and others join in soon enough. Then we move to something that just about anyone can do without complex directions or guidelines—a pencil or crayon work on drawing paper. The idea for the drawing could come from what happened in the circle, or it could be any other idea. As the teacher, I join with my new students, while having the opportunity to observe them. We share afterwards. I look specifically at each child's work and say what I see in the work right away. This might be a comment on use of color, presence of characters, placement of objects, use of line. I invite children to join in as I model this.

Other opportunities to better know the person arise from the very start of the school year. Norman comes up to me. (I notice that he has come up a great deal already, and it is only 9:00.) He shows me his latest drawing. My first impression is "scribble." I ask him about his drawing and find out that it is a story: pathways through a forest and something on the edge of the forest is about to get the boy, but he runs and hides. No wonder there are so many interweaving lines! The tendency to judge quickly reminds me of the importance of slowing down and looking at work together with a child.

FORMS AND SCORES

In the first moments of the first day of school, when we gather in a circle, we create a space to be together. What has been put off in order to make these first moments a time together? Forms. There are more forms to be sent home each year, many of which are purely administrative. These are not the forms that clash with my notion of what it is to know the child. The forms that disturb me are in purple file folders. They sit there in a filing crate not more than 6 feet from where we hold our greeting circle. In these files there is a pink sheet for each student with scores from last year's final assessments along with a sample of writing (scored by rubric), a sample of a Developmental Reading Assessment (DRA), the Developmental Spelling Analysis (a phonetic features list) from Word Journeys, and an assessment of math concepts from Math Perspectives.

I find it useful when a prior teacher sends along a range of writing samples, collected over time, and notations of books that interest the child. Pictures of pattern block designs, Unifix pattern strips, number books, and other student-generated materials, especially art work, also help in this getting-to-know process. If a work folder contains these things, then the materials in the purple folder can become part of a broader picture.

Thinking back on this now, I'm aware that starting in grade 2 the pink sheet with the scores will remain, but the actual supporting material will tend to thin out. That is because most assessment from the prior spring will have been done using criterion-referenced multiple-choice tests that the children take on the computer. As I pass on this year's children, I note that Carrie is a Fluency 5 Conventions 3 writer, a DRA 16 reader and a Letter Name 19 speller. The Math Perspectives material isn't reduced to a number, but once Carrie is in grade 2 there will be a number for math as well. This is why I am disturbed by the purple folders sitting next to my desk. The numbers are beginning to be the focal points at our school. Maybe they already are.

CHILDREN AND THE CURRICULUM

As I sifted through my files, I came upon these notes about my 3rd-grade class in November of 1992:

The wheels, pulleys, and chassis I pulled out of the science lab throw-away pile are a popular addition to the classroom. Ethan has created something huge. Brett and Sammy have been enthusiastic about this area as well . . . Sammy used his car as the focus of writing yesterday—taking the car apart to obtain angles for sketches he wanted to make, then putting it back together, and finally adding some writing below the picture.

Now, more than a decade after the time described above, I wondered if I would notice those chassis, pulleys, and wheels in the junk pile—especially if teaching in grade 3. That, after all, is the year when the state standardized testing begins—that summative testing upon which we as a school are judged. Even as a grade 1 teacher, I might not find room for that material—the physical room, yes, but room in the daily schedule?

Despite the pressure I felt in my school to conform to externally imposed standards, I knew that this had not been and could not be my starting place as a teacher. Instead, I expect that each person will make a contribution, and I ask early on and through the year, "What does this person bring?" In Alice's class, William brought maps and cities. Jen brought the power of description, especially using her sense of hearing. Tucker brought rolling balls and falling cubes—experiments in motion. Everett brought fantasy worlds. Reba brought nature studies, with her interest in close observation of the natural world. Laura brought still-life drawing, which worked wonderfully with Reba's flowers. David was our information hound; with the habits of a pollster, he gathered and compiled a great deal of data about the students in our room.

My friend Karen Woolf, who had just retired from more than 30 years of teaching, spent many days volunteering with us that year. Karen noticed the diversity and richness from the first time she entered our room—and she reminded me to listen for all of the children's stories. Every child brought stories, and many acted them out. No wonder we ended up with a play of our own making, a saga of the travels of an orange named Sir Robert.

The Sir Robert story did start with a lesson from the formal curriculum—health and wellness, in this case. The Sir Robert curriculum came to incorporate several parts of the regular curriculum—from writing (helping with play lines) to reading (the emails from Sir Robert, and play lines) to measuring paper for scenery to the geography of the Western Hemisphere (not really a 1st-grade curriculum standard, but . . .)

THE OFFICIAL VIEW OF CURRICULUM

My school's changed view of curriculum as something to be "delivered" didn't easily make space for the unexpected, the chance encounter between children and materials that can, under the guidance of a responsive teacher, develop into new curriculum ideas. In addition, a narrowing view of

assessment had taken hold, replacing a broader view that included looking at children's work. The criterion-referenced multiple-choice tests, taken
electronically two to three times a year, had begun as one or two times a
year, in grades 3–8. Now they had crept down to grade 2. I foresaw a future
of testing mania in which even kindergarten students would be frequently
subjected to these tests.

If assessment drives instruction, a mantra often repeated in our school
and others, then curriculum has become geared to only that which is assessed
through multiple-choice tests. The criterion-referenced tests were supposed
to guide our instructional decisions under imposed standards. Though individual schools or teachers might develop ways to creatively work with
these standards, leaving more room for children's ideas, I rarely saw this
happening at my school. The testing, the numbers, the gridding had come to
dominate. We pretty much took what was handed down.

CHAIR'S INTERLUDE THREE

*At this point I felt that I had a full enough picture of Bruce's teaching
and the conflicts he was experiencing to begin talking together about the
focusing questions for his Review and the headings that would structure it.
Once developed, these would guide the rest of the planning. The headings
for a Descriptive Review of Practice, unlike those for the Descriptive
Review of the Child, are worked out anew for each Review.*

*Drawing on the material Bruce had brought from his years of
teaching and his concerns about the changes afoot at his school, we agreed
that Bruce's struggle to enact his own values in an increasingly alien
environment was central. Now we would hone this idea to a question that
would be specific enough to elicit responses and recommendations from
participants in the Review. After some conversation, we settled upon this
focusing question: "As Bruce continues to work in his current situation,
what supports will help him strengthen his own descriptive practices in
the classroom and more effectively communicate these practices and the
thinking behind them to others?"*

*We then talked about how to organize the Review to enable participants
to understand his conflict fully enough that they would be able to offer
useful responses. We agreed that using the overarching tension between
Bruce's own values and what he calls the "official" view would work. Since
Bruce felt that was enough for him to work with, we didn't fine-tune the
headings at this planning session. However, we did note that the headings
needed to pull forward the conflict between the value he places on getting to
know each child well and on curriculum as evolving and participatory and
the "official" view of the child and of curriculum.*

The headings would serve to organize Bruce's description of his practice, but the heart of the Review would be the specific stories and examples he would bring to portray his teaching practice in its particularity. Since Bruce was already experienced with descriptive process, I didn't work closely with him on the selection process, as I would have done with a newer presenting teacher.

MOVING ON

After the planning meeting with Ellen, I put more thought into the headings. Drawing on ideas from our planning, I formulated six headings for my Review of Practice:

- getting to know one another in the classroom
- official view of the child in my school and my responses
- my understanding of how curriculum evolves
- descriptions of the range of curriculum in my school
- feeling tone of the classroom
- feeling tone of the school

I continued to prepare on my own by describing in greater detail the contrasts we had identified, using examples and stories from my teaching practice. Ellen and I corresponded over the next couple of weeks and met on the evening we arrived at Summer Institute to go over the plans and make any last-minute adjustments. Because it was summer, I was able to spend more time than usual preparing. If I were doing a Review during the school year—as is usually the case—I wouldn't have had such luxury of time, and the planning would have been more compressed.

As Ellen pulled out of my driveway on that July afternoon, I realized that just gathering up and reflecting on the material with my chair had given me a new perspective from which to view my situation. I was looking forward to presenting a description of my own teaching life that would open it up to others so I could begin to see it through their eyes. For all of us, there would be shifts of perspective and new questions raised.

PART III

The Art of Teaching

*Reflecting, Questioning,
Documenting*

Drawing on the same resources that inform a Review of Practice, teachers can examine their own practice and document classroom activities on a daily basis. This section provides accounts of the ongoing inquiries of two teachers who rely on careful observation, description, and documentation of children's ways of making sense of the world to ground their thinking about the classroom and as a practical guide to planning.

Lynne Strieb tells how she developed various kinds of teaching records that became essential to her understanding of children and her planning for their learning. Her chapter, "Drawing the Child Forward," shows how her observations accrue over time and how she uses her records to work with each child as an individual and to communicate with parents.

Kiran Chaudhuri's story, "Valued Work," extends an inquiry over time. We see her questions change as she tries new things with her students and how the responses she gets when she brings material to an inquiry group feed into her work with her class. Her inquiry keeps cycling back to a core question: What does it mean to have valued work, work that matters?

CHAPTER 8

Drawing the Child Forward
Keeping and Using Narrative Records

Lynne Yermanock Strieb

I've always been an observer and describer, at least since I was 7 years old, when I was given my first serious art supplies—a box of used pastels. I first copied greeting cards, then painted the farm outside my bedroom window. At 11, I began to sketch people on the "el," trying to capture their postures, gestures, faces. As a teenager, I became interested in describing in writing what people did. The questions that preoccupied me (in addition to "What do people have in common?") were "What makes people stand out as individuals, separate from one another? How can that individuality be captured?"

Holding onto experiences has always been important to me. Whether on family trips across country or working as a teacher, I wrote to remember. I believed that certain experiences were worth holding onto, and capturing them in writing was more meaningful to me than seeing them in photographs. The written record made it possible for me to remember and return to the event—to analyze, interpret, document.

INFORMING MY TEACHING, INFORMING OTHERS

I began to teach full time in 1970, and from then until 2000 I taught 1st and 2nd grade in three Philadelphia public schools. At that time it became important for me to write for several reasons. My "open classroom"—in which there was a variety of materials, in which children worked on projects, in which they could play with blocks, in which there was more noise and activity and less silence and sitting—was different from classrooms most of the parents had attended and most classrooms in my school. I had to inform parents about what the children and I were doing and what I was teaching.

I also wanted to remember what the children did, though the reason why was not fully formed in my mind. I believed that describing what I did and reading what I wrote would help me to become a better teacher, to raise questions that might further the children's learning, and to see if my students were learning from this way of teaching. I also wanted to remember what I was doing, just for the sake of remembering. I did not have a system or method in mind, and because I often tried to do too much, I was unable to make time to write on a regular basis.

My association with Prospect School and Center began in 1973 and continued throughout my teaching life. I felt immediately at home with Prospect's reliance on observation and description. Patricia Carini and the staff at Prospect School had developed several collaborative descriptive processes that gave me a systematic, disciplined way to organize my observations and descriptions. Edith Klausner, who was familiar with Prospect and a mentor in my early years of teaching, helped me to find a simple and regular structure for recording what the children were doing in class each day. Around this time, a group of us founded the Philadelphia Teachers' Learning Cooperative (PTLC), which was associated with Prospect. When we did Descriptive Reviews of children (Himley, 2000), we used our observations to describe the children's interests, to listen to various perspectives, and to collaboratively discover ways to build on the children's and teachers' strengths.

MY RECORDS AND MY PROCESS

I want to emphasize that I am recounting my own ways of keeping and using records. I'm a fairly disciplined person who likes to write, and as a result my records were extensive. However, I believe that all teachers can learn to observe and describe. While it is useful for teachers to keep records, to document the children and their own teaching, it must be done according to their own needs, time, purposes, and goals. Here's how it worked for me.

Daily Records

After school or at night, at meetings, or on public transportation on the way home, I wrote brief notes about what I could remember that a child did. I put these in my daily record under five headings: reading/language, writing, math, project time, social/emotional (see Figure 8.1). These notes were not meant to be complete. They were there to jog my memory so that later I

Figure 8.1. Daily Record

NAME: Ned Wynne

DATE: Tues. 9/10 to Weds. 10/2

Date	Reading/ Lang. Arts	Writing/Speaking	Math	Project/Choice Time	Behavior/Social
T 9/10		"r," "a" backward; knew abt. Monarch b/fly	2,3,4 backward	Lego	upset about choosing; afraid wrong choice
W 9/11		cont. dragon story; knows abt. mon. food	is rect. bec. 4 sides, 4 corners	clay—brief	Mom sent note
Th 9/12	can read, I think	cont. dragon		marble track	calls out—learning to hold back
F,M 9/13,9/16		butterfly	1–10		
T 9/17		sea ghosts; will continue tomorrow			
W 9/18		another kind of monster		hamster—loves animals	
Th 9/19			abs		

(continued)

Figure 8.1. (continued)

Date	Reading/ Lang. Arts	Writing/Speaking	Math	Project/Choice Time	Behavior/Social
F 9/20		knows letters are bkward		I like to . . . pattern blocks	
M-W 9/23–25		teeny figs.; detail; I say try wtg. story first		pattern blocks: symmetrical then paper	
Th 9/26				clay	
F 9/27	self–can read a lot	fighting cat		Lego	sometimes doesn't listen
M 9/30		dramatic: OH NO! Soon no trees	trip		
T 10/1	insect bks	see discussion abt. insects		blocks	mom in
W 10/2	animal bks	under the water story		blocks	

could write a more complete narrative. Because I was rarely able to write notes while the children worked (though many teachers can), I relied on my memory. Most days I was unable to put an entry into each of the five boxes, but over time the information built and a picture of the child emerged. If I had time for only one record, this would be the one I would keep.

Journal

After the summer of 1980, at the suggestion of Patricia Carini, I began to keep a teaching journal. I started because I had a question: "Where does the feeling lie in my classroom?" I thought I'd left no room for feelings, but if they were there, I might find them in whole-class discussions. Though I started to keep a record of only the discussions, by November of 1980 I realized how valuable the journal had become for my practice. The more I wrote, the more I observed in my classroom and the more I wanted to write. Rereading my journal led me to more teaching ideas. I expanded the journal to include other aspects of teaching—anecdotes, observations of children and their involvement in activities, interactions with parents both in and out of school, plans, descriptions of the pressures on public school teachers. I also wrote about my continuing education through my own reflections and the questions that emerged through books and through association with colleagues in the PTLC and at the Prospect Summer Institutes. I've kept a journal in some form or another since 1980.

I kept my teaching journal alongside my daily record as I jotted daily notes about each child. My journal was a simple piece of loose-leaf paper that went into a binder when the day's entry was complete. Writing the daily record reminded me of things I wanted to make part of my journal: things that had happened in the class during that day, things I wanted to reflect on further, things that seemed important about children (individuals, small groups, the whole class), things that I might not want to share with a parent about a child but that were important to remember. My journal was also the place where I made plans for teaching, based on the daily records and previous journal entries. Writing phrases or sentences in both the daily record and the journal took about half an hour each day.

Narrative Records

The daily records were exactly that—records. I felt that I needed to take those "raw" records and analyze them to discover the patterns of each child's interests, learning, approaches to classroom tasks, and social interactions over time. Using my daily records, I wrote narrative accounts on two children per night, in a 3-week cycle (30 children). Additionally, I sometimes inserted information from my journal in a child's narrative record. When I began to write narrative records I was characteristically too ambitious. I tried to write narratives on six children each night, that is, 30 children in one week. Edith Klausner came to my rescue: "Give yourself permission to write about 30 children in 2 weeks, three children each night." And many years later, she urged me to give myself 3 weeks to complete the class. "You have all the information, so it doesn't matter how often you write the narrative," she said. Writing about two children each night took about 20 to 30 more minutes. It was to these narrative accounts that I turned when I wrote reports to parents or prepared for report card conferences.

Over the years, as we in Philadelphia were required to give 1st- and 2nd-grade children A, B, C, D, F grades on their report cards and to give standardized tests, I relied even more on these daily and narrative accounts to inform parents of what their children were doing and learning in school. Parents appreciated the detail and insights that these records made possible. Many times I was told how much more they learned both about their children and about what was going on in the classroom from my accounts than from grades and test scores. This is discussed in more detail in my article, "When a Teacher's Values Clash with School Values: Documenting Children's Progress" in *Exploring Values and Standards* (Andrias, Kanevsky, Strieb, & Traugh, 1992).

Student Work

I kept each child's work in a folder. I looked through it carefully to find themes, motifs, and evidence of change and progress when I wrote narrative reports. For example, when reading a child's writing, I noted the child's interests, themes, motifs in the content, and changes in understanding of the conventions of language. I sometimes noted whether or not the themes in the child's content played out in other activities in which the child participated. I observed what the child created during Project Time (a time when children could choose from among a variety of materials and activities), again to see where the child's interests lay. I showed parents their child's work during report card conferences, and we learned about their child's progress by looking at it together.

Communication with Parents

Inspired by a parent newsletter from Prospect School, I started writing a biweekly newsletter to parents in 1971 and continued this practice until I retired from teaching. Writing that newsletter was my first successful attempt to inform parents of what we were doing and why. These newsletters also served three additional purposes: They were a location for inviting parents into the classroom and then thanking them for their help; they informed the principal of some of the things going on in my class; they were a good reminder for me of what the children and I had done together—a record of curriculum.

From 1996 to 2000, I saved all the notes and letters of substance that parents wrote to me. This was an excellent way to learn what sorts of things were on parents' minds, which I discuss in more detail in *Inviting Families into the Classroom* (2010).

Class Discussions

I began to record class discussions in writing in 1980 as part of my journal. At first I recorded them by hand, but later I was able to use a laptop computer. After school, I proofread the discussions, printed and copied them, and, the next day, put them into homework books for the children to read with their parents. I assigned the children to watch for their names and to learn to read what they had said. The next day, we would read the discussion as if it were a play script. It was a way for me to give the children something that they'd really be interested in reading (their own words) and to let parents know some of the things we were doing in school. It allowed me to remember things we'd talked about. Reading the discussion was an excellent way to see children's ideas about science, literature, and social matters and to learn about their language. It also helped me know the nature of individual children's contributions to those discussions.

DOCUMENTING ONE CHILD: NED

I recount here the story of how my observations and descriptions of one 6-year-old, Ned Wynne, helped me to work with him and communicate with his parents. I draw on my records from September until early December, a time when his parents brought some concerns and questions to my attention.

Ned's Parents' Concern

On October 21st, I received a note from Ned's mother: "Bob and I have some things we'd like to discuss with you about Ned, and would like to meet. . . . Please let us know what your busy schedule would allow. Thank you for all your efforts on behalf of the kids. It's clear how much work you put into the children's learning experience." The note also included the following postscript, which gave me further insight into Ned: "P.S. As Halloween approaches, would you please excuse Ned from any 'scary story' time? He becomes *quite* scared. Thanks."

Because I tended to get nervous when parents requested a meeting but didn't tell me why, I wanted to meet as quickly as possible. From my journal:

Later in the day I had a chance to talk briefly with Ned's mom. She began by telling me that Ned is very verbal and so he tells her everything. He has complained of being bored in school and is feeling he is not being challenged. I was surprised about this and immediately felt that I must be doing something wrong (Isn't that *always* my first reaction?). . . . We set up a meeting for November 4, during which we would talk about this matter. Meanwhile, I told Ms. Wynne that I would think about this, and I promised to pay attention to Ned to try to discover what the issue about boredom is really about.

Early Observations of Ned

I looked back through my narrative records from the first few weeks of school, where I had described the ways in which Ned stood out to me. On October 2, I had written:

Ned can read, though he mostly looks at nature picture books. He loves animals. He has learned the names and life habits of many insects and other creatures from books he has at home, and he eagerly shares this knowledge in class discussions.

Most of his writing is about him fighting with imaginary creatures—dragons, monsters, sea ghosts, a cat. The stories are one sentence long, usually. His drawings are very detailed and filled with teeny figures. I'm trying to get him to write his story first, then to draw the pictures. It's taking him so long to get the writing/drawing done. I've been working with him on the letters that he writes backwards.

At Project Time he spent a long time observing the hamsters. He loves animals. When he worked with pattern blocks, he made a flat, symmetrical design, then he used the animal paper, putting pattern blocks within the outline.

Ned can be very dramatic. When we were at the Balch Institute, he said, "Oh no, what are we going to do for air if they cut down all the trees?" He worries about these world-shattering issues. At the beginning of the year he was upset because he didn't know what to choose: "I'm afraid I might make the wrong choice." He got over that quickly.

Preparing for the Meeting with Ned's Parents

I continued to observe Ned and to describe in my daily records what he was doing, what he was interested in, what he observed and seemed to be learning or having trouble learning. In my journal I noted:

I have noticed that at quiet reading time he usually chooses books that are about his major interest, animals. . . . He and his friends usually choose books with interesting pictures and with text that is rather difficult and beyond their growing ability. They enjoy talking about the pictures and are never bored with the detail.

I also noted that Ned was a competent beginning reader, that he used mostly phonics to decode words, but sometimes lost the meaning of the sentence as he tried to figure out a word. Continuing, I wrote:

It is when I ask Ned to take some time to try reading easier fiction that he seems unhappy. I think that all he needs to do in order to become a more independent reader is to read, which will give him lots and lots of practice. When I asked him directly about what is boring, he said that he doesn't like quiet reading time, something which surprised me. . . . He also said that writing time is boring.

I had noticed that Ned usually wrote one sentence each day and drew a picture. The following story took him about 10 days to write:

My Trip to New York
   by Ned Wynne
I went to New York to see my friends Jacob and Brad.
I played on their computer and I went to the New York Zoo.
I stayed there for two and a half days.
When I went to the zoo at New York I pretended that I was
      a prairie dog.
At the New York Zoo I saw a bunch of mircats.
At the New York Zoo I saw a macaw and I saw a snake.
At the New York Zoo I saw a baboon and I saw a praying
      mantis and I saw an owl.
In New York one of the computer games was called
      Jazz Jack Rabbit.
At night I slept on an air mattress.
Then I left and I had a good time.

Over the years, with more than 30 children in a class, I had to develop conference rituals around writing that were not completely satisfactory either to me or to the children. I divided the class into two groups. Each day, as half of the children completed their daily writing, they lined up to wait for their conferences with me. Because Ned worked quickly and wrote one sentence at a time, this wait could indeed be boring.

The Meeting with Ned's Parents

My meeting with Ned's parents was cordial, and they seemed to appreciate my hard work. I asked them to talk more about Ned's complaint about being bored and about Ned at home. Just as I had observed, Ned loved learning facts, especially about animals. He enjoyed collecting information and could remember what he had heard. I had been sending home easy fiction and the easiest nonfiction about animals that I could find. Mr. Wynne said that his son was resisting reading those books. Ned wasn't interested in the fiction, and he couldn't get the information from the nonfiction quickly enough because it was too difficult. As a result, he was insisting that his parents read to him only the books filled with information.

I had listened to Ned reading *The King's Wish*. I believed it was a good book for him because he knew most of the words, and it would give him good practice. I told his parents that reading sometimes seemed to tire him and when he read it to me he wanted to stop before he completed the first chapter. Nevertheless, when Ned first read the part about the King Test, he became interested. When I asked him to explain the King Test, he happily read that portion about five times to get it straight. He was then able to retell the story quite well and was pleased. I described writing time and the problems around the conference procedure. I thought Ned might be bored because he was finishing quickly and then either had to wait for others to finish or had to wait in line for a long time to have a writing conference.

I told the Wynnes that I knew from class discussions that Ned knew many facts about animals and had acquired knowledge that would probably continue to interest him throughout his life. I mentioned some things that I might do at school and that they could consider doing at home. I would encourage Ned to spend a little more time writing each day—and perhaps to write more than one sentence—and asked his parents to remind him to do the same. This would allow him to spend most of his time writing, rather than waiting. I said that although I couldn't possibly give Ned (or any of the children) the attention they might want or get at home, I would attempt to find ways to feed his interests. I suggested that they might be able to compromise with Ned on reading the books I sent home: Perhaps they could take turns with him, each reading a little.

Back in the Classroom

After talking with Ned's parents, I began to insist that Ned read some easy fiction at school and take whatever he had been reading in school home to read to his parents. He had just finished reading *The Big Jump* and did a good job of retelling the story to the class. His parents told me that they were much happier now that he was reading to them at home. He continued to love informational books and learning facts, and I believed that he would soon be able to read some of the easier nonfiction independently. I also noticed that Ned was spending more time writing. By December, I had found Ned some easy nonfiction books about whales, sharks, and manatees. He told me he'd been reading them with his parents, but then, after a while, he slipped back into reading familiar, very limited vocabulary, easy readers like *Snow*. He continued to have trouble in school settling into reading and finding a book that interested him. He also continued to want to look at animal picture books that interested him, without getting the practice he needed in reading. I seemed to be asking him to read independently when he was simply not ready to do so.

Something else happened in early December that I recorded in my narrative records and journal and described to Ned's parents in his December report card:

> Recently I asked Ned how Quiet Reading time could be more interesting to him, and he told me he'd like to learn about creatures. Though he couldn't think of one he'd like to learn about, he did narrow it down to mammals. He sat for three Quiet Reading sessions, sorting all the mammal books into two piles: those with animals he wants to learn about, and those he wasn't interested in. His concentration was remarkable. We then sat together and further sorted the book into content that was similar (rodents, felines, etc.). I told Ned that I'm happy to have him read about animals, but that he has to choose books with words that he can actually read by himself. His choice was a book about animals with pouches, and he is on his way. . . . Now he is writing everything he knows about African animals, which I will encourage him to "publish."

Gradually, Ned began to read more independently, and he saw that he was allowed to write about things that interested him. In observing Ned's interests and in being attentive to his growing ability to read, I was able to provide him with materials and activities that supported his ways of learning. Ned stayed with his class and with me through 2nd grade, and I heard no more complaints about being bored in school from Ned and his parents.

IMPLICATIONS

My observations and descriptive records gave me detailed and specific information about the children I taught, information I relied on in making teaching decisions. However, description is generally dismissed as "subjective" by state and federal departments of education and school districts, whereas numerical evidence from grades and standardized tests receives official sanction and is promoted as "objective." Actually, these tests are no more objective than description. Items on which test scores are based are written with a predetermined purpose in mind. Believing that tests give objective information about children can narrow a teacher's focus to what is tested. Description is more useful because it has the potential to widen the lens through which teachers look at each child. In addition, through description a teacher strives to portray the distinctiveness of each child, whereas test scores, in their standardization, render the person invisible.

For a teacher to be able to describe each child, she has to find ways for individuals and their work to stand out. I found that a classroom with a variety of materials, activities, and choices made it possible for me to note what each child did and knew, how he or she approached the activities, and what his or her interests and strengths were. It is difficult to describe children with specificity when everyone is working on the same thing at the same time. When I taught whole-class math lessons and everyone did the same follow-up (say, a worksheet), I had trouble grasping how a child was thinking and whether the child understood the work. As a result, my math records of whole-class lessons were not especially informative. In contrast, records based on my observations of children working at math activities and with materials at Project Time gave me lots of information about what they knew.

Although description is bound to be subjective, there are ways to guard against being arbitrary or substituting judgment for description. Over many years of teaching and working with colleagues at the PTLC and Prospect, I became increasingly aware of the importance of using language in my daily and narrative records that I would feel comfortable having a parent read. This was brought home to me after I'd written that a certain child was "babyish" and, thinking that my records were OK for parents to read, had shown them to his parents. The parents were terribly upset by my choice of that word and I had to explain what I meant, using specific examples. Even with the explanation, it was not a good word to have used. That experience led me to examine more closely my use of such words as "wild," "babyish," "smart," "slow," and "interesting." It taught me that instead of finding one word to sum it all up, I needed to be more descriptive. If I choose a word to describe a child—in narrative records, narrative report cards, or in conversation with parents about their children—it is important that I follow that word with examples, specific incidents or samples of work that supply the evidence for the descriptive word.

I have learned over the years that description acts against generalization. Reflecting on my observations about how Quiet Reading Time wasn't working for Ned led me to open a conversation with him that gave him entry to reading for his own purposes. My response was particular to Ned. It wouldn't apply to other children, but I could count on my records to provide specific information that would help me work with each child as an individual. My records, based on observation and description, made Ned (and the other children) more visible to me—they drew forward the interests and strengths of all the children.

CHAPTER 9

Valued Work

Examining and Reexamining Teaching Practice

Kiran Chaudhuri

Looking up from conferring with one writer, I scan the classroom's lively activity, and note how others are engaged here, now. Astonished, I feel a rush of exhilaration; or, dismayed, I panic. Inhaling sharply, I exhale and steel myself to notice more. Have I provided students with the time, space, choice, and materials that they need to make and do things they value? How can I make space for this valued work? How can I make it visible to colleagues? At the end of the day, pulling gum and candy wrappers from inside the desks, retrieving dictionaries and erasers, and seizing a first draft tossed into the garbage, I regroup. I plot adjustments and prepare differently. I go back in the next morning to see how these changes, small or big, impact kids' learning.

Teaching thrusts me into relationship, and puts me in the way of opportunities that I must seize or forfeit, opportunities that determine whether I serve or fail my students. It challenges me, ready or not, to trust—to trust in human capacity, to trust that adolescents' choices lead to learning, to trust myself. It insists that I examine my values at their root, that I value different perspectives, that I value adolescents' own standards for their work. It engrosses me in observing, collecting, describing, documenting.

Teaching draws me forward, craning to get a closer look at a student's work, then allows me to step back to see the person and observe what he or she is doing in context. Conferring with a student about his or her writing prompts me to reach for language with which to describe back to the writer what it is I observe. In the process, I notice craft moves the student is making that I hadn't seen before. Meeting with colleagues, I find myself straining to describe what I just observed in the work. Writing alongside my advisees in our end-of-day journal reflection and, after school, emailing colleagues who share the same student, I document how what I've been describing today jostles interpretations I'd previously made. Having created processes for students to perform and exhibit their work, I hope this student's publishing will enable all of us teachers to see what this writer is doing from another angle.

I teach 9th grade English and Advisory at East Side Community High School, a public 6th- through 12th-grade secondary school of 500 students. I begin and end the day with Advisory, which is focused on social and emotional learning. My two English classes each have 23 students and meet for 2-hour blocks daily. The school is located on New York's Lower East Side and largely serves families from the neighborhood. Ninety percent of our students stay with us from grades 6 through 12. The majority of students are Latino (60%) and African American (35%). Ninety-two percent are eligible for free- or reduced-price lunch, and 20% are the first in their families to graduate from high school. Ninety percent of our graduates go to college, and 75% are first-generation college-goers.

This story evolved as a series of reviews presented to my school, to the New York City Adolescent Inquiry Group, and to the Prospect Center's Annual Conference. These reviews included Descriptive Reviews of a Child, a Descriptive Review of a Child's Work, and a Descriptive Review of Activities in the Classroom with Implications for Knowledge-making, Learning, and Curriculum. It is a story still evolving, likely to continue to unfurl with the help of another review.

CONNECTIONS WITH MY OWN LIFE AND THINKING

The classroom hums. Students are absorbed in doing or making things that they—and I—find meaningful, experiencing what it's like to have "work that is done for the love of the work itself, work done to benefit others, work that fulfills desire through the disciplined pursuit of a medium" (Carini, 2001, p. 90). In her essay "Poets of Our Lives" Patricia Carini writes of work that "creates its own world, governed by a rhythm that, breaking stride with the relentless march of measured time, transports the worker" (Carini, 2001, p. 45). Whether they are playing chess, discussing a primary historical document, drafting a poem, or editing a narrative, I want students to lose track of time, ignore outside forces that buffet their attention and let go of self-consciousness. Having valued work contributes to the growth of a sense of self and to an adolescent's emergence as a person. When classroom conditions allow for the person to come forward in this way—as maker and doer—others are more able to recognize her for who she is.

This envelopment in valued work is something I get when I am writing, reading, practicing tae kwon do, and even teaching. It was something I got as a kid working on school projects. When I was 12, I spent hours mounting an insect collection. Every day after school, my sister, our best friend, and I lugged our clothes hanger nets up the hill and down to the fields, where we ran through thistle and Queen Anne's lace, netting cabbage butterflies and bluebottles. We shook them out into jars we had filled with ethyl-alcohol-soaked paper towels and whirled around again to catch a gypsy moth or a dragonfly. We ventured down lesser-known paths in the woods, kicking over damp logs, shrieking at armies of beetles that surged forth, laughing at each other until we gasped, and the sun set, and the trees got ghostly and we hurried home. Sprawled on the floor after dinner, I extracted the insects and pinned them carefully into a blue shirt box. Glancing back and forth between guidebook illustration and specimen, I identified and labeled each one.

I would like to say that my stance is one of "joining-with and following-after," as Lillian Weber suggests (Weber, 1997). Too often, I get in my own way. Still, there are moments when I succeed in making expectations clear and attainable and in structuring activity so as to enable myself to confer with individuals and groups. It's then that I can notice when students are "onto" something, and I provision time and materials that both support and challenge their interests. I am prompted to design curriculum that is open ended and to support individuals in shaping assignments for themselves. I can establish a relationship with them around their work—valued work—and an authority that is authentic and sought after, like that of a coach or master craftsperson.

Valuing absorption in meaningful activity, then, leads me to value choice and adolescents' own standards for what they do and make. It leads me to seek out authentic occasions and audiences for assessment. It leads me to visit early childhood and elementary classrooms to study how children learn. It raises questions. How do you structure adolescents' interaction with materials to enable valued work to take hold in the classroom? How do you support a 15-year-old in meeting external standards without squashing the standards the students themselves hold for their work?

AN INQUIRY TAKES ROOT

The starting place for my inquiry was an anxious question: What do most early adolescents need in order to learn and grow? I was starting a new job teaching 9th graders Humanities at East Side Community High School. I had taught Humanities to 12- through 21-year-olds in various configurations and had just spent the summer reflecting on what I'd learned from describing one particular 13-year-old, Nile (Himley, 2000). Basically, though, I'd taught early adolescents just enough to know that I didn't know much. I knew I needed to ground myself amidst the swirl of new experiences with 13-, 14-, and 15-year-olds. I decided to do a Descriptive Review of a Child.

When school opened, I bought a bound notebook in which to keep the year's inquiry notes and chose Ben to observe. He was a boy whom the school had decided to hold back in the 9th grade. His work folder was accumulating pieces of paper with a few lines written, but no completed assignments. He would write an insightful reading log every Thursday in After-School Homework Help, but he was not doing any other homework. I noticed that he wrote poetry in a battered composition notebook, leaning against the gym wall between basketball games during lunch hour. When it came time to sign up for a studio elective, he chose to continue work he had begun the year before in the Poetry Studio. In Independent Reading, he would regularly pull out a library book from the mass of crushed papers at the bottom of his book bag. In class discussions, he would offer an idea about the novel we were reading that would prompt others to ask questions that were closer to the text. Given time, he wrote a memoir that, when I hung it outside the classroom, stopped passersby. The more I observed Ben, the more I saw that, despite failure to be accountable to certain school standards, he was "onto" something of his own.

Our Humanities class went around the corner to the Tompkins Square Branch of the New York Public Library to choose independent reading books. Ben chose *Death, Lies, and Treachery* (a Star Wars comic), a how-to book that teaches you how to make interesting sounds with your mouth, and *Dragon War* by Laurence Yep. Four days later, I asked Ben which book he had chosen to read first. He said he'd read them all and gone back to exchange them for more. He opened his book bag and pulled out two new books, *Amalgam Age of Comics* and a Marvel Comics graphic novel, and started to read. Later, when our Advisory was playing Two Truths and a Lie, one thing Ben told the group was "I have read over two thousand books." The kids guessed that this was no lie. When his classmate Rafik interviewed him about his reading, Ben responded, "200," to the question, "If you had to guess, how many books would you say there are in your house?" To "How did you learn to read?" he answered, "My mother taught me." He listed Stephen King as his favorite author. A whole-class discussion got going about books we'd enjoyed, with everyone piling in after Ben contributed, "*The Big Book of Urban Legends*. That book was phat." The next day, I brought in *Pissing in the Snow and Other Ozark Folktales* and put it on the shelves. Before I knew it, he had spotted it, walked over, and reached for the book, murmuring to himself, "Look! Look at this! Urban legends!"

In October, still concerned about Ben's difficulty completing assignments, I presented a Descriptive Review of Ben at a meeting of the Adolescent

Reading Inquiry Group. My colleagues reflected back to me that it was plain to them that Ben was learning. I agreed to present the review more fully at the Prospect Annual Conference. In November, I presented a description of Ben's work to my school's staff. Linette Moorman, my chair for the conference review, helped me to weigh what I'd observed most recently together with the perspectives and recommendations I'd gathered from colleagues at the two previous reviews of Ben. My question became: How can I help Ben appreciate his own strengths, and use them to take on challenges in assigned work as well as independent work?

One result of this process of returning again and again with various colleagues to what I was seeing in my classroom was that I became bolder in questioning my assumptions about production and work. Was it so important that Ben produce evidence of his learning? Does a person have to be working to produce evidence in order to be learning? What is work, anyway? What does evidence of nontangible learning look like? Do you need evidence at all?

Entering this phase of questioning made me glad that I had set up Independent Reading for the first 30 minutes of every Humanities class. I had different standards for this portion of my curriculum. I was more concerned with noticing what kids were doing (reading!) and how they were doing it than with assessing. It was a time when Ben could learn without necessarily having to produce. East Side Community teachers had resolved the June before to have Independent Reading in all Humanities classes, grades 6 through 12. Having found setting up independent reading to be daunting before, I took it on as a challenge, almost as another inquiry project, alongside my study of Ben and his work. By December, these two inquiry projects were merging. The perspective I'd gained on Ben's modes of thinking and learning and the questioning stance that I'd developed in describing him were confirming my ideas about the power of time and choice in the Independent Reading curriculum.

In my last year at my previous school, I had recognized the need to put an independent reading program next to the whole-class reading program I had in place. Facing Andrew's, Javier's, and Melanie's reticence to read, I thought the choice of topic, author, language, genre, length, and level of reading that independent reading allows, as well as the peer pressure to have a book, might support them to take on the challenge.

Over the summer, I had dipped back into some of the theory that had guided me when I was beginning to teach. I pulled Louise Rosenblatt's *Literature As Exploration* off the shelf and thumbed back to her comment that "the really important things in the education of youth cannot be taught in the formal didactic manner; they are things which are experienced, absorbed, accepted, incorporated into the personality through emotional and esthetic experiences" (Rosenblatt, 1989, p. 181). She advocated for providing the student "with as broad a gamut of literary experiences as possible. Even more important is the scrupulous effort to avoid any academic procedures that may hinder a spontaneous personal response" (Rosenblatt, 1989, p. 274). She asserted that reading—active reading—develops "the imagination: the ability to escape from the limitations of time and place and environment, the capacity to envisage alternatives in ways of life and in moral and social choices, the sensitivity to thought and feeling and needs of other personalities" (Rosenblatt, 1989 p. 290). These ideas resonated with a remark of Maxine Greene's that I ran across in my lecture notes, about how aesthetic experiences—such as reading—could make adolescents "more present to their own choosing." James Britton offered the term "wide reading" and advocated fostering it "side by side with close reading" (as cited in Thompson, 1987, p. 243).

Given East Side Community High School's strong support for Independent Reading, I decided that the kids and I should have a free-ranging choice of books for our personal "wide reading" in the first 30 minutes of each 2-hour block. Our "close reading" would involve reading as a whole class or in book clubs, as well as writing about that reading, talking about that writing, and listening to each other's responses. This year our books would be *When I Was Puerto Rican* by Esmeralda Santiago, *Taste of Salt* by Frances Temple, *Nectar in a Sieve* by Kamala Markandaya, and *The Good Earth* by Pearl S. Buck, all supporting our study of imperialism and resistance.

EPISODES AND TELLING MOMENTS

In September, I waded into setting up Independent Reading. By November, I noticed signs that some of my students had a reading life and that what we were doing in the first 30 minutes of class had value for them beyond school. Kids were asking, "Can't we read longer?" and "Can I go to the library? I finished my book." I noticed that we often read quietly together past the time I'd allotted on the agenda. My teaching journal began to accumulate entries like these:

> Lea and Jade locked in a tug of war over a copy of *Beloved*; Julio eyeing Alejandro's thumb in the last pages of *Rule of the Bone*; Alejandro leaning over Julissa and Emily's shoulders to read *Changing Bodies, Changing Lives*; Chrystal snatching *Changing Bodies, Changing Lives*. Absorbed in her reading, paying no mind to the hullabaloo she's causing. She better give it back now or . . . OK, she gave it back. How do I get that hum of strong calm in here if I also want kids to be socializing over their books?

Emily looking over Ben's shoulder at *The Big Book of Urban Legends*. He gave it to her. Always the gentleman. Alejandro came and sat next to her, turning the pages. Ben left it on the bookshelf at the end of the period, saying it's for anyone else who wants to read it. But it's from the Tompkins Branch Library. He said, "I can afford the late fee." What!!? What if they walk off with it? His grandmother doesn't have money for that. Maybe he's basking in the younger kids' admiration?

Drown—Juan read it, but I have no idea yet what he made of it. He didn't write about it at all. But reading, it's like playing an instrument or like painting. It's enough in and of itself. Why should they have to write about what they read? I don't do that, generally. Julio tried it but it had to be too hard for him. Finally returned it. How do I steer kids away from books they can't read and toward books they can?

Kiana signals to me across the serene circle of readers that she wants to read from her book at the end of Independent Reading. I nod and turn the page of my novel. Does this mean that they're getting it—how to do book talks? Launching book talks has been harder than I thought with these younger kids. A student taking initiative to share from her book, even scheduling it in advance? Could Kiana be giving it a go? When she reads from the chapter of her book *Girltalk* on menstruation, her face cracks a delighted smile; Sameer and Rafik sink down in their seats uncomfortably, rolling their eyes. I hold my breath and glance at my student teacher. He seems calm, not catching my stricken look. I decide to trust author Carol Weston's reassuring tone. I know that Independent Reading is one of the more porous places in my curriculum, offering space for students to infuse Humanities with the stuff of their lives, making what goes on in my classroom a little closer to home. I don't want for our talk to transgress the boundaries of safety for anyone in the room. But sexuality so dominates 13-, 14-, and 15-year olds' attention, and we find so few entry points for it in the close reading portion of our 9th-grade Humanities curriculum on imperialism and resistance. At the end of her reading, I thank Kiana and comment how surprising it is to learn that menstruation depletes your calcium and lowers your blood sugar. And how amazing it is that, even as Independent Reading throws us together in a circle, it allows us to travel to far flung——and here I search for words, and Louis supplies—"realms."

How to make Independent Reading a time when we travel to our own private imaginative worlds and then bring a bit of these back into the classroom and the curriculum? How to make the hard edges of the public soften? How to make the classroom intimate, when we're all reading something different? How to enable kids to spiral out of their independent reading into projects of their own, given our thematic inquiry?

ASSESSMENT AND DESCRIPTION: QUESTIONS AND ISSUES

I reveled in these moments of my kids' engagement with books and worked out my own standards for students' learning, but I was also worrying about the issue of assessment. How can I assess what they are learning? If they are not discussing their books, don't they need to be writing something about them so that I can see some demonstration of their learning? What about Ramses, who is fidgeting, chatting, staring down at the page, staring out into space? Is he reading at home?

In addition to this desire to find out what was going on in my kids' reading lives, I also had to set up grading measures. One grading instrument I made was a wall chart, with a row for the books read by each member of the class. I wrestled with the question of whether the competition it would set up would prove counterproductive to my goal of helping kids to enjoy reading. My 1st-grade teacher had had such a chart, but I had disliked it. It made me feel less smart than a classmate who read one more book than me. On the other hand, I thought, it did motivate me to read more books. Perhaps it was "healthy" competition. What's wrong with a little peer pressure around reading? I decided I would try it and listen for feedback from the kids.

It turned out that the kids never talked with each other about the chart. A few kids talked with me about it, reminding me to add a book they'd just read. The rest of the class seemed to pay it no mind.

At the start of the second semester, I tore down the chart and began documenting their reading using Nancie Atwell's Status-of-the-Class Reading Record (Atwell, 1998, p. 109). I walked around the circle, writing down each student's page number. It enabled me to check in with individuals about how they were reading, when, what attitudes and feelings they had toward their reading. "How do you like the book? Read me a paragraph," I would whisper.

Assessing this way helped me to see that one of the other measures I'd set up also needed transforming. I had arranged for my students to correspond about their reading with lawyers from a local firm. I noticed that what the pairs wrote about the books was thin and wondered whether the letters were really helping the students see more about themselves as readers and get a glimpse of another person as a reader. How could I help them write more reflectively about their reading experience? I decided to be more deliberate about teaching response in connection with independent reading, to help kids transfer what they were doing in the close reading to what they were doing in their wide reading. I designed a guideline sheet for students to use in writing their letters, listing four techniques they recognized from doing annotations and dialectical notes on their close reading: React to a paragraph with your feelings, make a prediction, make a connection, ask a question. This elicited complaints. Annotation and dialectical notes are ways for a reader to act as spectator to his or her own thought process, to slow down reading enough to chart the movement of the mind as one reads. Yet perhaps doing this does wreck Independent Reading. My purpose with Independent Reading was to provide time, choice, materials, structures, and models for becoming a person who likes reading. The new assignment was not serving that purpose. In fact, a hollow note of compliance crept into letters and their postscripts: "My teacher told me to quote a chunk that caught my eye, so here goes . . ."

I dropped the new campaign and stepped back even further. I asked myself what kind of writing do *I* do about books I have read. Not much. I started to wonder, how do you collect evidence of intangible work? What constitutes evidence, anyway?

In March, I presented a description of student work to my adolescent reading inquiry group by way of trying to figure out what to do. I brought the pen pal letters and some portfolio cover letters, memoirs, and essays referring to independent reading. Embarrassed at how little evidence of reading the work captured, and how secretly bored I was with reading pen pal exchanges, I was surprised to hear inquiry group members note matter-of-factly that such letters generally are more about the "pal" than anything else. I came away seeing that it was not a matter of my professional adequacy but a matter of problem solving. I needed to try a different form and audience: The kids needed to be writing to their peers. Then they would invest the energy they were putting into creating relationships and building community *within* the classroom instead of without. And they would be involved in documenting the verbal and nonverbal conversation flying across the reading circle. The inquiry group recommended that I keep documenting the interrelationships among kids, between the kids and me, and between their wide reading and their close reading. They recommended that students might gain more from exchanging letters with the adults about their close reading than about their wide reading. Relieved, I decided I'd substitute dialogue journals for pen pal letters. I bought notebooks on the way home.

Perhaps I—and the kids—needed not evidence but a collection of "vestiges of that daily life" surrounding their reading, to use Patricia Carini's words (Himley, 2011, p. 50). It was an "ah-ha" moment for me to see that collection need not be for portfolios—for hard evidence, for proof, for defense—but could be, rather, for observing, describing, and gaining an understanding. Collection could be for documenting the ecology of literacy in my classroom. Collection and description could become much more important than assessment.

But I didn't want to discard self-assessment altogether. I still wanted my students to be asking themselves, What did I get out of all this effort? What did I learn? So what that I learned it? What does it tell me about how I've grown as a reader and writer? As a person? What do I want to try next? Shaunte did a bit of this in her memoir, writing about her interest in books about girl characters she could identify with. Julissa wrote a section of her portfolio cover letter about how her book choices this year were all about sexuality and gender. I decided that the next year I could have kids create annotated bibliographies as they read, including title, author, publication information, genre, the story of how they got hold of the book, what made them want to read it once they did, and excerpts from their dialogue journal entries about it.

Having set up dialogue journals for kids to share their responses to Independent Reading books with each other, with my student teacher, and with me, I was excited when I noticed them reflecting on their reading without being evaluative. Juan wrote about how he "loses the story" whenever he allows too much time to go by before getting back to his book. Rachel, Kiana, and Alicia wove questions about their own gender and sexuality in with talk about that of characters. Louis and Alejandro wrote back and forth about war books they'd found worth reading, and Ben and Kevin laid plans to go to the public library after school to get more super heroes comic books.

It was a blessing for me to have a way to establish a journaling relationship with Kevin, Juan, Saul, Janine, and other reluctant readers. I was stumped where I noticed Emily and Ramses writing about everything but their reading. Reading these pages in their notebooks reminded me that I needed to write in each of the books—maintain a presence in them—so that kids keep them for a public audience, rather than falling into the trap that Kiana and Adulfo had earlier in the year—flirting, directing personal questions, and making disclosures.

Regardless of whether I was excited or stumped by what they had written, they had created a record of their response to their reading that I could study. The more I could step back from snap judgment into a descriptive stance, the more I could begin to trust adolescents to make meaning in their own ways.

My practice with adolescents keeps growing, in large part a "grappling," as Lillian Weber calls it, with what it means to take a descriptive stance rather than a judging stance. "The path of constant reexamination, of grappling-with that assumes no final end or conclusion or perfection in any of the settings, is a feature inherent in being a teacher" (Weber, 1997, p. 179). Descriptive inquiry has an astringent effect on my work, toning and clarifying. In the Descriptive Review circle, the group of participants helps me to recognize larger patterns and to reevaluate my assumptions, beliefs, and values.

Making Room for the Child

Recollecting Childhood, Valuing the Child's Perspective

In Part IV, we hone in on the child's perspective. At Prospect, recollection has always been an important resource for teachers that enables them to connect to the children they teach. As teachers become ever more sensitized to their own lifelong perspectives, they can also look at children with more sympathy and understanding for particular, perhaps unusual, ways of thinking.

In "Recollecting Play," Francesca Michaelides Weiss juxtaposes memories of her own childhood play with glimpses of her students on the playground. She is prompted to attend to play by her feeling that "in schools, play has become suspect." Louisa Cruz-Acosta, in "Worlds Apart, Worlds Together," contrasts her memories of growing up in a bilingual Puerto Rican household with her childhood experience of school. She recognizes that her history at home and school made her "conscious of the harm that is done when people are denied the expression of their own languages and cultures."

Each of the next two stories begins with a child who puzzles his teacher. In "Trusting Aidan with Math," Regina Ritscher writes about a child who solves complex math problems in his head, but has difficulty explaining his thinking. Ann Caren, in "Paying Attention to Justin," describes a boy who initially has difficulty with math assignments. Through systematically observing these children and documenting their observations, these teachers gain insights that offer them a wider lens, which leads to new approaches to working with each child.

CHAPTER 10

Recollecting Play

Its Meaning Then, Its Message Now

Francesca Michaelides Weiss

When I attended a leadership forum, I was one of very few teachers in the company of corporate leaders representing the likes of American Express and Starbucks. We heard stories of corporate executives working to humanize the workplace through reflection, collaboration, and yes, play.

In one session we were asked to play with Legos as an aid to articulating our notions about leadership, life challenges, and values. The 60 or so adults jumped at the opportunity to play. I saw in adults what I have witnessed for more than 20 years in my work with children: engagement and focus, creativity, pride, and enthusiasm as structures were shared. There was laughter around the tables as adults messed around with Legos.

I couldn't help thinking how ironic it is that while these corporate leaders are being encouraged to use play in their workplaces, schools are eliminating recess and curtailing options for play in the classroom. The corporate leaders acknowledged play as a path to insight and learning, whereas in schools, play has become suspect.

THOUGHTS ON PLAY

I have come to realize that my ideas about play have been shaped by my own experiences as someone who used to play. Now that I am middle aged, I realize that I have spent many more years not playing than playing. My own culture, as I was growing up, informed me that play was frivolous and something to be put aside in adulthood. As the years passed I was left with a feeling of loss.

I worry that children will not have enough time for play—that the real world will take over soon enough and that they too will have spent so many more years not playing than playing. I can remember that when my own children were little I was constantly opening the back door on fine days and saying, "Go play!" On snowy days it was, "Let's put your boots on and bundle up and go play." And they did.

I tell myself that the more time children have to play in their own ways the better able they are to work out relationships and the human problems that arise when interacting independently with their peers. I tell myself that through play children are connecting more richly to their inner lives. They enact their dreams and fantasies, become their favorite TV, movie, or story-book characters, and take on the conduct and responses of those who are models to them. How else do children learn to become men or women than through pretending to be their teachers, mothers, fathers, and other adults they see in the world? How else do they learn about heroism than through pretending to be heroic in rescuing another child from the "bad guys"? How else do children learn about fairness, sharing, suffering, pain, and tenderness but through the empathy experienced in play? I tell myself that play is a way to practice being a person within a social group without the intrusion of grown-ups. I tell myself that through play you get to try on roles for size, to find out how they feel and if they fit.

With all of this in mind I go about trying to give my children in school as much play time as possible. Most days, my K/1 class goes out twice a day for about 15 to 30 minutes for each recess. This is apart from the 15-minute recess given during their lunch period. But in making that decision I have added a new anxiety to my life at school. If children are spending more time playing, then they are spending less time doing something else, such as reading or writing or math. It opens up a whole new Pandora's box, filled with concerns about standards, expectations, and accountability.

Nonetheless, I became convinced by observations of children at play that, despite these concerns, the children needed more time to play. In the children's play, I saw their creativity, inventiveness, and engagement with each other and with ideas, and this affirmed my commitment to play as the important work of children. Though we try to encourage children to articulate their thinking and their ideas in the classroom, adults actually spend much more time asking children not to talk, except within structures such as shared reading, conferences, meeting time, or small-group work times. Recess periods allow children to explore possibilities in relationships, play out conflicts, and build strong friendships. Children use language spontaneously and freely through their play. They use their voices, imaginations, and energies as they explore and make meaning of their world.

For all I can see of children's play, there is much that remains invisible to me. I think the things I don't see are of great importance. I think that the children make some of their play invisible to others because it is often so deeply personal and compelling.

ON THE PLAYGROUND

Kaylee

I see Kaylee struggle on the horizontal bar of the outside equipment. She comes to me to say that it is so hard and that she wants so much to be able to just hang on without falling to the ground. And so each day Kaylee practices. First she is able to hang suspended a foot off the ground until she drops. Then she is able to swing her body before letting herself go. This year she is working on swinging arm over arm on the horizontal ladder. With each triumph there is a confidence and an exhilaration that are visible in her face. She is practicing running now too. On the heels of the summer Olympics it became her wish to be an Olympic athlete—to run fast and smooth and win a race. She and some other children sprint from one end of the yard to the other, and everyone wins. Everyone is an Olympic champion.

Under the Equipment

I see a cluster of children, three or four, huddled under the equipment in a dark, sheltered space where only children this small can fit. I cannot hear them. They whisper and giggle and point to each other and plan and I am not permitted to be a part of that. Sometimes the children take chalk or pencils and pieces of paper with them into that space. They seem to be making lists or writing messages.

Running

Sometimes I watch as children just run, and run, and run. In the early years of my work with children I used to wonder why the children would just run. I'd open the doors, and the children would fly out and race across space. I'd worry and ask myself, "Why aren't they playing?" They would whoop and holler and throw their heads back and run like mad. I came to see that space, open and wide, is so limited for many children. So many children do need to just run.

Treasure and Trevor

Some children look for treasure in the dirt and collect it. They find small stones, lost beads, or pieces of colorful paper that have been blown into the yard by the wind. More recently the children gathered twigs to supplement the set of Lincoln Logs that we have in the classroom. Before our toad Trevor died, the children dug for worms and bugs that they thought Trevor would like to eat. Then while they were at it they built small hills and mountains and discovered lost buttons to add to their treasure, and they buried seeds.

Talk

Sometimes children want to hold my hand and just talk. A different kind of talk than the talk that takes place in the classroom. There is no expectation of being entertained or instructed. It's just having a chat.

Chalk

Some years ago the principal of our building banned chalk from being used outside in the yard. When our school hired a new principal, nothing was said about chalk, so the K/1 teachers quietly brought it into the yard and hoped for the best. The children made hopscotch boards, wrote their names and their friends' names, drew various kinds of pictures. Just before the holidays the children began to draw a line. They drew a continuous straight line from one end of the yard to the other, taking turns. You could see the little breaks where one child left off and another began. The children got a little stuck when they got to the end of the yard. They couldn't turn a corner, so they went back to the beginning and drew a parallel line. They made about five of those.

Over time the line-drawing fad took new directions. Children drew lines independently, so that the yard resembled a street map with lines curving, turning, and intersecting one another. I was invited to walk their lines and follow the paths of different lines. Other children joined in walking the lines to see where they would lead and if they would diverge or if a different line could be picked up and taken. New lines were made from old ones, and that play continued until the snow came.

RECOLLECTION

I remember going to church as a child. We attended a Greek Orthodox Church and the rituals of the services seemed so filled with mystery and a comfortable kind of darkness. The church itself was very old and there were a lot of places or spaces that seemed to share this same comfortable darkness. And I remember that we kids knew all the places and spaces and that we thought of them as ours. I'm guessing now that the grown-ups were equally aware of these places, but we didn't think they knew. We had this sense that the spaces belonged wholly to us.

As an early childhood teacher, I think a lot about what the children will remember in the future. It seems to me that people remember the sense or the feelings that some things were really personal and really theirs. I remember a lot more about the special spaces in that old church than I do about the schools I went to and their spaces.

I am always thinking about what things we provide that will last as food for the soul well into adult life. I care a lot about what people will remember. I think it matters.

I'm not sure if there is more I should do to provision for children in outside play. They seem to bring most of what they need to this play themselves. It seems to me that what I offer the children in terms of outdoor play is not necessarily structure but boundaries. Boundaries that are big, yet safe. Boundaries that are large enough to help children suspend disbelief and become lost in time and space. Maybe the best thing that I can do, especially in these times, is just open the back door.

CHAPTER 11

Worlds Apart, Worlds Together

Memory as Catalyst

Louisa Cruz-Acosta

"Lo que uno aprende, nadie se lo quita."
("What one learns, no one can take away.")
—*Abuela*

I can still remember snippets of my first day of kindergarten in a Brooklyn public elementary school in the 1950s. My mother had accomplished the impossible. A piece-worker in New York City's garment district, she'd been given the day off from her factory job so she could escort me to school and meet my teacher. I vaguely remember being at once nervous and excited. On the morning I was to begin my formal education we walked hand in hand the four long blocks to a large red-brick structure. As we approached, we saw parents standing outside the enormous metal gates at the school's entrance.

Children were being ushered into the building by several adults, including a tall, imposing figure with a gleaming bald head and broad smile. We would soon learn he was the principal. He greeted everyone with a warm smile and then, politely but firmly, he dismissed the parents. He told them that the children would now begin the process of learning how to make their own way through the corridors of the school. When my mother attempted to persist in her effort to meet my teacher, she was curtly reminded that her presence was no longer needed, that it would, in fact, hinder my adjustment to school. And, he added, she ought not to coddle or "baby" me further by insisting on coming in.

I have no memory of how I got there, but once I arrived at my class-room somewhere on the second floor, I was surprised and delighted to see a familiar face. I discovered that my neighbor and best friend's younger sister, Magda, was one of my new classmates. Just as quickly, however, that feeling turned to anxiety as I witnessed her first encounter with our new teacher. As soon as she was greeted, Magda turned to me and burst into tears. She could not understand a word of what was being said to her. To the teacher's dismay, the more she tried to console her, the louder Magda cried.

As I witnessed that first encounter, somewhat frightened, somewhat relieved that it was not with me, I can still recall a sense of urgency to do something about what I was witnessing—to help in some way. Fortunately, thanks to my mother and grandmother, I had learned to speak both Spanish and English, so I could communicate with both my new teacher *and* my friend.

On that occasion, the teacher was grateful, but after their initial interactions, many of my attempts to help Magda and the teacher to communicate were rejected because, it was explained to me, she needed to learn to speak English and "the sooner the better." Back on our block, I began to notice how Magda grew increasingly withdrawn. She was also often absent from school. This experience has stayed with me, as painful experiences sometimes do. To this day, I often feel that same compulsion to take action when I witness someone being misunderstood or mistreated because they speak a language other than English.

Most of my memories of those early school experiences are of children seated in rows of desks with a perceptible distance, a kind of gulf, between the teacher and the children. That distance, a deliberate demarcation, ensured that there would be no ambiguity about the difference in role and status of the teacher and the students. The adult, the teacher, was at a "safe" distance in a way that kept her in charge and in control. In one case, an elderly teacher, a seasoned veteran, had gone as far as placing a line of thick, black vinyl tape between her desk and the classroom door. Whenever children entered, they were to wait behind that line to be acknowledged before they were permitted to address her.

I have all-too-vivid memories of how some children were treated as "good, smart children," how they were singled out as the teachers' favorites. These children often enjoyed special privileges and were given a certain amount of authority and responsibility. They were sent to do errands and allowed to serve as class monitors, while others were frequently ignored or treated as untrustworthy, even undesirable. Eventually, I came to understand that all too often these distinctions followed the rigid racial and socioeconomic stereotypes found in American society at that time. Some of these distinctions persist to this day.

FAMILY MEMORIES

I was the older of two girls born to a fair-skinned, college-educated Puerto Rican mother and a dark-skinned Puerto Rican father who had gone to school through junior high school. While they grew up in very different home environments with different kinds of school experiences, my parents were both from racially mixed families who were devoutly religious. They often spoke to us about their belief in basic human equality and the importance of respecting people for how they lived and treated others, not for how they looked, where they came from, or what material possessions they owned. Living these values at home and having them reinforced at weekly church services was a powerful formative experience for me. Consequently, I became increasingly disturbed by what I witnessed throughout my years in the Brooklyn public schools of the 1950s and 1960s.

At the time, most children in New York City attended their local neighborhood schools, so the schools' student populations reflected the surrounding community's demographics. The local public school I attended from kindergarten through 6th grade was located in a section of Brooklyn called East New York–Brownsville and was a few city blocks from our small, one-bedroom apartment in a four-story walk-up tenement. The neighborhood surrounding the school was largely made up of working-class Puerto Rican, Jewish, and "Negro" families; therefore, the school's student population was racially mixed. However, there were very few people of color working as teachers in New York City's schools at that time. In my school, the teaching staff was White and female; the two administrators, White middle-aged men.

My home and school were worlds apart. I was largely raised by my mother and her older sister and enjoyed regular contact with members of my father's family who had migrated to New York City in the 1950s. My maternal grandparents, back on the island of Puerto Rico, also became important role models for me. My grandfather, who had graduated from high school, was one of only two postal carriers hired by the U.S. government on the island and was, therefore, able to provide well for his family during my mother's childhood and young adulthood. He was an eloquent, passionate man who had many interests and hobbies. I liked hearing the tales of how, after a long workday, he enjoyed breeding roosters and writing short stories and poetry. My grandmother—a master storyteller, cook, and seamstress— was a proud homemaker who devoted her life to caring for a large extended family. My relationship with my grandparents was a driving force behind my desire to complete my education. Along with my mother and aunt, my grandparents taught me about Puerto Rican history and culture.

In 1950, my mother, the first in her family to attend the University of Puerto Rico, moved from her childhood home to New York City in order to complete a bachelor's degree in the natural sciences. A very loving, strict, and disciplined parent, my mother believed that at each stage of development, children were already fully formed people with experiences and interests of their own. She thought they deserved to be treated with respect and spoken to with the assumption that they could understand and communicate complex thoughts and feelings. She insisted that we be aware of the significance of our decisions and actions—even at a young age.

As far back as I can remember, my mother and her mother, my *abuela*, instilled in me a fierce pride in who I was and where I had come from. Their insistence that I learn Spanish and speak it regularly allowed me to communicate with all my family members during visits to Puerto Rico. Though she visited us in our small apartment in Brooklyn almost every summer, my *abuela* spoke only Spanish. "Therefore," my mother reminded us, "you and your sister *must always be able to speak Spanish* so you can communicate with your *abuela*."

Abuela loved to reminisce. I looked forward to hearing her stories about her personal and family history whenever she came to visit. The tradition of telling family stories and singing and dancing with children at home was passed down to my mother and her siblings, so I grew up hearing richly textured family stories from many different perspectives.

One of my favorite family stories is about *Abuela* awakening my mother and her many young siblings before dawn on summer mornings and walking several miles to meet the sunrise on the seashore. *Abuela* had given birth to 12 children in all. The first three did not live past a few months. In addition to caring for her own children, *Abuela* took in and raised her two nieces when their parents were no longer able to care for them. On those early summer mornings, *Abuela* prepared for the day by packing up blankets and food. "It is very important to take the children to the water," she would say, "because there is much to learn there and the water is very healing." I think of this every June when the children in my class and I pack food, towels, sand toys, and rubber slippers and board a school bus to spend the day at a local beach.

RULED BY NUMBERS

At my school, the grade number was followed by a hyphen and a designation from 1 to 6. The number after the hyphen was a ranking: the higher the number, the lower the rank. As I grew older, I realized that the children in the lower-ranked classes were considered to be less intelligent and more difficult to teach. Often students remained in these same groupings until they graduated from grade school. The group designated by the number 1 was almost exclusively made up of White children, while the children in classes ranked 2 through 6 were mainly Puerto Rican and "Negro." This system had an effect on everyone in the school. Children were often labeled"smart," "good," and "bad." I overheard teachers talking about children, using these narrow, demeaning terms. This system served to rank teachers as well, with new teachers or teachers out of favor being assigned to the "bad" classes.

I was moved around among these class designations throughout my 7 years at the school. In 1st grade I was assigned to Class 1-3. The following year, I was moved to Class 2-2. Initially, this made it difficult for me to figure out what group I "belonged" to and how I was being perceived by the teachers. Therefore, though I felt smart, important, and loved when I was with family at home, for many years I doubted whether I was "smart" or "good" enough to pursue higher education and a professional career, because I had not been considered part of the "top" or "number one" group during elementary school.

By 3rd grade I figured out that there was a system for placing the "good" children in the "good" classes and that it was the "good" teachers that usually got them. That year, I found myself in Class 3-3, reunited with many of the children I started out with in 1st grade. But that year I'd also gotten lucky. Miss Ruben, a new teacher at the school, was young, energetic, and outspoken. She possessed several qualities I appreciated. She was smart and kind to us much of the time. She was fair and even funny. Miss Ruben never wrote kids' names under a big letter "X" if they "misbehaved," a common practice in our school. She encouraged the participation of all her students by calling on children who raised their hands to speak in class, regardless of their race. She often read aloud to us and even engaged us in conversation. She did many things that were unusual for teachers in that school, such as taking our class on trips. That spring, she took us on a tour of New York City landmarks and places of interest I'd never seen before, even though I'd lived there my entire life. We visited places like Fraunces Tavern, the United Nations building, and Chinatown and were able to see firsthand some of the many different kinds of people that lived in our city. Even though I was in the number 3 class, I knew I was lucky to be one of Miss Ruben's students.

Other aspects of the public school experience became evident to me that year. For example, I learned the importance of the seat you were assigned to in class. In many public elementary schools of the time, classrooms were organized in rows of wooden desks and chairs that were placed side by side with very little space to move in any direction. The location of your seat was important because it was an indication of your place in the group and it affected your access to other children. That year, I became aware of the fact that there were children of different races in the class and that they were segregated. Generally, the front-row seats were saved for White children, while "Negro" and Puerto Rican children were relegated to seats in the back of the classroom, furthest away from the teacher. I quickly understood the real significance of this arrangement: There was a direct correlation between your location and the kind of relationship you could have with your teacher. That year, to my surprise and good fortune, I had been assigned a seat in the front row, next to the teacher's desk, for the first time since I'd started school.

On my last day in Class 3-3, I cried, even though my report card said I had been assigned to Class 4-2. I cried because I knew that I would probably never see Miss Ruben again. I would miss all the interesting things we did and learned about that year. I would miss her too, even though she'd said, "I wouldn't believe you if you stood on your head and spit dollar bills!" to Stanley, the "bad" Black boy in the class who sat in the row closest to the back of the room.

In 6th grade, I finally made it to Class 6-1. When I proudly announced the great news to my mom that evening, I didn't know what a solitary experience it would be. I was the one new person in Class 6-1 and the only person of color.

TAKING HOLD

Years later, when I became a parent, I was determined to give my children access to a richer, less biased, and more child-centered educational experience. I drove them several miles south each morning from our apartment in the Bronx to a small alternative public school in East Harlem, called Central Park East I (CPEI). I had heard about CPEI from a close friend whose son would be attending. Not until I visited the school did I see the kinds of classrooms I had only read about in college textbooks.

At an orientation for prospective parents I had noticed how carefully the classrooms were provisioned. There were hundreds of books in multicolored bins all around the rooms. There were plants and class pets: gerbils, rabbits, and turtles. Children sat together at small tables and sewed, painted, wrote in notebooks, and read books. All this activity was occurring simultaneously, producing a pleasant and continual buzz of children's voices. As we toured the school, I saw children engaged in a wide variety of hands-on learning experiences: reading books and writing their own stories, playing math board games, working with computers, engaging in dramatic play, and conducting experiments. I knew that day that I was witnessing something unique.

On my son's first day of kindergarten at CPEI, the parents were welcome to join their children in the classroom. As we all sat on the floor, I watched and listened as the teacher, a young Black woman whom the children called by her first name, spoke directly to the children about what choices would be available for them that morning. *Choices*. That was the word she kept repeating. As I observed the teacher throughout that year, I realized that she believed in giving children an active role and responsibility for their own learning. I came to understand that in offering opportunities for choice she was creating a classroom with entry points for all learners, one where everyone could become visible and well known to each other, including the teacher.

Eventually, with encouragement and support from many other teachers and friends in the Central Park East community, I entered the teaching profession and adopted this child-centered way of working with children and their families. In 1993, I joined a group of teachers and parents to establish the Muscota New School. It was part of a network of small, progressive public elementary schools in New York City, some of which still exist today. Muscota is located in a racially and socioeconomically diverse section of upper Manhattan known as Washington Heights/Inwood and is modeled after the Central Park East Schools and Prospect School. At least 60% of Muscota's student population has always been from Spanish-speaking families. While Spanish and English are the main languages spoken by Muscota's families, there are families whose native languages are Mandarin, Hebrew, French, Italian, Swiss German, Russian, or Arabic.

I have been a classroom teacher at Muscota for many years, teaching 6-, 7-, and 8-year-olds in a mixed-age, 2nd- and 3rd-grade class. My personal history both at home and in school made me conscious of the harm that is done when people are denied the expression of their own languages and cultures. For this reason, although my class is not technically a bilingual education class, we often incorporate the use of both English and Spanish in our daily rituals and whole-class meetings. Every sign and chart in our classroom appears in both Spanish and English, and our class library contains books written in a variety of languages. In this way, children who are just learning English can continue to acquire essential knowledge and skills in the content areas as they learn a second language. For English-speaking students, this practice has had the added benefit of facilitating their learning of basic Spanish and even some beginning Spanish literacy skills.

All the materials I send home are in Spanish and English, so that Spanish-speaking families are informed and included as partners in their children's education. My monthly family letters are written in Spanish and English, with the Spanish text appearing first. The idea for this practice came to me in my second year of teaching. One of my students, Elisa, had arrived in New York as an infant from a small town in Mexico. At our very first Family–School Conference, Elisa, her father, and I sat at a table with her drawings and work displayed before us and talked about how well she was learning in school and how proud we were of her progress. Just as we were about to end our conference, Elisa's father suddenly looked at me and said sadly that his daughter no longer wanted to speak Spanish at home. He explained that it had become a real problem because the child's mother only spoke Spanish. Elisa not only refused to speak to her mother in Spanish, she told her that her mother too should learn to speak English like Elisa and her father had. He then asked me to help Elisa understand how much harder it was for her mother, who stayed at home to care for her baby sister, to learn a new language.

It became obvious at that moment that I had a particular kind of responsibility to this child and family and an opportunity as well. As her teacher, I was in a position of authority, an agent of power representing the dominant culture. If *I* didn't speak Spanish, even though I could, why should she? I have incorporated the use of different languages and cultures in my teaching practices ever since.

THE STRUGGLE CONTINUES

Though there have been many attempts to restructure and reform the New York City public schools since I was a student in Brooklyn in the 1960s, the system remains largely as impersonal and stratified along racial and socio-economic lines as it was when I was a young child. Current efforts to reform this persistently troubled system are most notable for their familiarity: Children, families, and teachers are judged by narrow standards based upon the premise that "one size fits all," and progress is almost exclusively measured by standardized test scores. With increasingly high stakes attached to test results, schools are under pressure to implement policies that they think will raise test scores.

A direct result of these policies has been to further segregate and marginalize the very people they were supposed to help: the children of the working poor, of immigrants, and of single parents. Privileged students are segregated from those who are less privileged. All too often, schools that serve poor children adopt programs whose sole purpose is to drill children on testable skills, at the expense of providing an education that stimulates them to raise and investigate questions.

At the Muscota New School, we teachers believed that the results of the state-imposed standardized tests yielded limited and, often, skewed assessments of a student's ability and potential. Therefore, the significance and impact of these test results were minimized by teachers, students, and most families. Instead, teachers developed and implemented a rigorous system of multidisciplinary assessments, guided by age-appropriate learning expectations and ongoing observation. These were used to continually tailor teaching to individual student needs. However, over the course of almost 20 years since the school opened its doors to the diverse racial, cultural, and socioeconomic community it serves, its basic principles have reflected a slow but steady change toward the structures imposed by legislative and local government mandates. Accommodating to those demands and pressures became necessary in order to survive, but even in the face of these external pressures the school was able to hold onto its mission to honor racial and cultural diversity.

In many other schools that serve large numbers of immigrant children, however, there are English-only policies, and some states even have laws restricting the use of languages other than English in schools. Because language is one of the most powerful tools of assimilation and acculturation, English-only proponents make a strong case for teaching English as soon as immigrant children enter school. But assimilation comes at a great cost. To deny a person's culture and language is to negate a person's very essence.

When I got involved with Prospect in the 1980s, I was immediately drawn to the way in which teachers were encouraged to draw on memory as a source of understanding of both self and others. Recollection is one of Prospect's descriptive processes, and it is often used to enter a topic and to explore its meaning in the lives of participants. Sharing my own memories and listening to those of others has given me a renewed appreciation of the power of memory, as well as language and culture, to inform our understanding of others. As I listen to the recollections of people with life experiences different from my own, I find myself entering their worlds, crossing boundaries of culture, language, race, and class.

What I have experienced and witnessed as a child, a parent, and a teacher has confirmed for me how vital it is that children be encouraged to communicate in the language they know best, the language of the family. I am haunted by my memories of Magda, in tears, surrounded by a language she couldn't understand. My recollections of my own childhood—of family stories heard and learned in Spanish, of the gulf between home and school, of the ranking of students that reinforced ethnic and racial biases—inform the choices I make as a teacher. The urgency I felt as a 6-year-old, watching Magda's humiliation, is with me still. It lives on in my commitment to continue making it possible for each child to bring his or her inner life—interests and experiences, language and culture—into my classroom and my school.

CHAPTER 12

Trusting Aidan with Math

Challenging Expectations

Regina Ritscher

After 20 years as an elementary classroom teacher, I have become a math enrichment teacher for grades 3 through 6 in a Boston-area school. I go into classrooms, involving children in inquiries into mathematical thinking and problem solving. I also meet with small groups of children who are thought to have mastered regular classroom lessons. While some students attend these once-a-week groups all year, the grouping is kept flexible, and many children move in and out of them depending on both what is being taught in class and the project I am offering.

Working with a 3rd-grade class, I notice that Aidan sits slouched in his chair, which is pulled out so he can barely reach his desk. As I stop to talk with him, he sits up slightly, tilts his head to look at me, and tells me that 1 × 22 and 2 × 11 are the only ways you can package 22 candies (Burns, 1991). When I ask him how he figured this out, he explains that he "just knows."

Aidan's "just knows" stops me in my tracks. I haven't worked with him much, other than encouraging him to get out materials, to become engaged in the investigation at hand and, at times, to find a partner. He is present in the whole-class explorations but rarely contributes to our discussions. His teacher tells me that she thinks he understands math but won't do the work, that he is lazy. My observation is that when he does speak he usually has the correct answer.

To determine what students know, we often rely on them to explain the process they used to solve a problem. This emphasis is apparent in current math curricula: the goal of helping every child to explain his or her understanding is explicit throughout the National Council of Teachers of Mathematics *Principles and Standards for School Mathematics* (NCTM, 2000) and reflected in the frameworks developed by individual states.

Emphasizing explanation leads to teaching activities in which children are expected to show their thinking and to a focus on class discussions and math journals. It results in classroom assessments—as well as state and national tests—that require that students explain their strategies.

My interaction with Aidan causes me to reflect on the tie between verbal knowledge and math that such activities assume, and I am disquieted. Not all mathematical thinking can be easily verbalized, and Aidan is not alone in his frustration when asked to do so. Many eminent mathematicians and scientists express how difficult they find it to articulate the means they use to solve problems—Einstein and Feynman come immediately to my mind. Award-winning mathematician and physicist Roger Penrose describes his own mathematical reasoning to be accompanied by "inane and almost useless verbal commentary" (Penrose, 1989, p. 424).

"JUST KNOWING" MATH

Working with Aidan through much of 3rd grade and all of 4th, I realize that he is, indeed, interested in math, although he continues to sit silently on the sidelines until the work becomes very difficult. When given the choice, Aidan leaves the easier problems to his classmates and begins with the complicated ones at the bottom of the page. When I ask the group to make up more problems, his are extremely complex, involving numbers in the thousands, which he then manipulates in his head. If there is noise, he is distracted and arrives at the wrong answer. Mostly he, amazingly, presents the correct answer with confidence and pride but no awareness of how he gets it. As I allow him to work on the "hard stuff" that interests him and ask him how he gets his answers, he gets interested in tracing his own processes. Larger numbers and more-complicated problems seem to slow down a thinking process that often happens too quickly for him to grasp—otherwise it is that Aidan, as he says, "just knows."

Given a Continental Math League problem that asks how many of his 24 balloons Bill would have to give to Betsy, who has 18, in order for her to have twice as many as he does, Aidan realizes that Bill has to give Betsy "a lot" and begins with 5. When this doesn't work, he immediately realizes that Bill gives her 10. Aidan has no explanation as to how he knows it is 10 but is sure this will work.

In 4th grade, I observe Aidan as he works on making a large 5 × 12 or 6 × 10 rectangle out of pentominoes (flat shapes, each made up of 5 square units connected in different configurations). Aidan sits in a corner of the room, again slouched in his chair, nearly at eye level with the pieces on the table before him, his hands in his lap. He reaches up to place a piece or two and then returns to watching. While the investigation began with students making rectangles involving smaller numbers of pieces, Aidan never creates smaller rectangles but comes closer and closer to making "the big one" as time goes on. Other than occasionally reporting that he now has only "one [pentomino] left," he works silently, ignoring his classmates—he is alone with the pieces.

OBSERVING AIDAN TO UNDERSTAND HIM

As I observe Aidan, I wonder what ideas and ways of manipulating numbers make sense to him to allow him, for example, to move from 5 balloons to 10. My trust that he does just know is founded on years of teaching and observation of children and adults, reflection, and study of thinkers such as Dewey, Bachélard, and Merleau-Ponty. Having studied with Patricia Carini and others at the Prospect Center and participated in many Descriptive Reviews of Children (Himley, 2000), I assume that knowing always has a pathway to it, a process of thinking things through that an individual relies on, and that I can come to understand a child's thinking better through observation and description. Because I want to understand Aidan's particular way of thinking, I do not limit my observations to math class.

> Aidan is quiet in class, his chair pulled back from his desk, while his body slides almost under it—as if he is looking for something inside. He seems less-than-responsive to what is going on around him, almost sleepy.
>
> Aidan's voice is quiet and even—when he speaks; he often shrugs when called on.
>
> Even when sitting with a boisterous group at lunch he watches, eyes flashing, but rarely speaks—joining in the silliness through action and giggling instead.
>
> Aidan is more active on the playground; in 4th grade, he is involved—as are many of his peers—in daily football games; again he is quiet, standing to the back of the group and watching the action. He watches the knot of boys playing, moves along the back of the playing area, and races into the fray after the ball.
>
> By the end of 4th grade, he occasionally gets excited about something he knows, as he does in explaining the balloon problem. On these occasions his voice rises in pitch, and he stands, leaning slightly forward, although his hands remain still.
>
> Only in the second half of 4th grade does he volunteer that when he was younger he had worked with his father on math and that he has known various math concepts for a long time. He expresses surprise that others don't know these.

His interaction with me over the candy-packaging problem begins
with his eyes: He turns his head and looks sideways at me as he tells
me that there are only two ways to package 22 candies. Aidan also
uses his eyes to communicate—glances that wonder if I see what he
sees, if I "get it," share it, and appreciate it.

When I think of Aidan's just knowing, I think of how he watches. His
eyes play an important role in how he gains information and expresses
himself. He seems to recognize how things go together and what fits or
works or looks (maybe feels) right. An example is his work with tooth-
pick-moving puzzles:

> He solves all of these without trouble: looking at the toothpicks,
> reaching out and moving one, carrying out what he sees quickly and
> confidently. A couple of weeks after he solved them, I challenge him
> to see if he could remember what he had done and if he could still do
> them. He could and did. Aidan looked at each problem on the page,
> recalling what had worked from its physical location in relationship
> to the others and then what he did seemed to come back as a whole,
> again with the confidence of "getting it." He did, rather than spoke.

Aidan's quiet, internal staring makes me think he is "seeing" processes
that aren't easy for him to articulate. He struggles both to verbalize his
understanding and to defend his thinking in the face of the algorithms his
teachers expect but that, he finds, increase his chance of misstep and error.
In spite of his deep interest in and fluency with the manipulation of space
and number, he runs into difficulty with external rules and with organizing
his work in ways that are visible to those around him.

When I allow him to begin with the hardest problems, he sometimes
makes what look like random marks as he thinks. Over the course of the
year he explains that these marks show steps in his thinking, and he begins
to tell me why he has trouble conveying what he knows during class pre-
tests—often lack of time or trouble with formats and laying out his work
in an orderly way. He and I also become aware of the holes in his understanding of the algorithms being taught, caused by his distaste for these
processes, as well as the frequent "careless" errors that are often the result
of his becoming distracted in the midst of complicated mental calculation.
He gets lost in the step-by-step procedures his teacher favors, makes errors
in calculation, and prefers shortcuts that he can work out.

By 4th grade, Aidan enjoys being noticed as "good in math"—by me
and also by fellow students. He also begins to pay more attention in the
classroom—to what his teacher is asking of him and how this does or
doesn't make sense to him. She notes that he seems livelier and happier.

ASSESSMENT AND TRUST

Observing Aidan and reflecting on my observations leads me to think about how math is taught and assessed. The traditional approach of teaching algorithms and procedures didn't work well for him, because they didn't make sense to him and he got tripped up by the steps he was supposed to follow. Providing him with a certain richness of material, complexity of topic, and time for exploration engaged him and allowed him to approach problems in his own way. It also made it possible for me to see what interested him, what he considered important, and how he approached new challenges. However, the expectation that he show his thinking didn't work for him. Unfortunately, many assessments rely on this sort of communication. They aim to inform a teacher about how children are thinking about mathematics, but they assume that mathematical thinking and verbal communication go together. As my observations of Aidan illustrate, this is not always the case.

The discrepancy between the assessments' appraisal and my observations stems from, in part, what is valued as mathematical knowledge. Today's assessments are carefully constructed; they no longer value only product—correct answers—while ignoring a child's processes. However, they continue to limit validation to reasoning that is clearly articulated to make sense to the evaluator and that proceeds logically from one point to the next. Yet, it is hard to accept this standard when Penrose describes his own mathematical reasoning as accompanied by language such as "that thing goes with that thing, and that thing goes with that thing" (Penrose, 1989, p. 424). Assessments favor precise terminology and explanations of organized processes, while the idea of "goes with" suggests a sense of working with the mathematical symbols that is almost concrete, a process of doing that can't necessarily be named precisely. Understanding mathematics in this active sense helps me accept that toothpick puzzles might be remembered through location and that if 5 balloons doesn't work, one might realize with certainty that 10 will.

Assessments may inform me about how well my students carry out particular tasks, but it is respecting and trusting their own approaches that helps me teach them. It is important to value and respect their preferred ways of knowing, rather than pushing them to immediately take on new and "better" ways. It is a matter of fostering engagement, of giving children time, space, and materials. Teaching, then, means paying attention to what each child is doing and his or her ways of figuring out and interacting with the world.

CHAPTER 13

Paying Attention to Justin
Small Changes, Big Strides

Ann Caren

Justin was a large child, tall and heavy, who entered the classroom quietly and soberly, with a hint of wariness. His eyes were alert and surveyed the classroom, but his face was expressionless. After I got to know him, I found him quick to smile, and then his face would light up, but I didn't see much of that in September. He moved slowly and when it was time to sit on the floor in the circle for class meetings, he sat a little outside the circle and almost never volunteered anything. Sometimes he would sit next to a friend from 1st grade and they would giggle and laugh together over some private joke. He was not responsive to my requests to "pay attention" to the discussion and often I asked him to leave the circle and sit at a nearby table.

The first time I remember hearing about Justin was when the school librarian, a colleague and friend I had worked with previously, said to me, "I'll be interested to see what you think about Justin." Her tone was one of genuine curiosity, but often when a teacher says that to another teacher, there's a hint of some difficulty with the child in school. Although I like to know about the children as learners and thinkers before I begin to teach a new class, I am not interested in hearing a list of deficiencies. So I took her comment as curiosity, didn't ask any questions, and started a new school year planning to get to know Justin as a person. I was new to Belle Sherman School and I didn't know any of the children assigned to my 2nd-grade class.

We had math early in the morning. The lessons started with the whole class seated together in a circle, the children next worked with a partner at tables, and finished by coming together in the circle again, sharing the solutions to problems or investigating some question that came up during the work time.

Justin usually had trouble beginning his partner work. At first, I wondered if he didn't understand the instructions or the problem or just didn't have any way to begin to work on the mathematics. Often his partners found him uncooperative, or if he were partnered with a friend, they would play with the materials, laugh, and tell stories.

I worked with a half-time collaborating teacher in my class. Mrs. Liddy was a competent and experienced teaching assistant who had worked at the school for many years and had worked with the children in our class when they were in kindergarten and 1st grade. She knew all of the children very well and her role had always been to give assistance to children who were in need of "remedial instruction" as part of the Title I program. However, our school was redefining how to provide support to children in academic subjects, and as teachers we were learning to work together to provide for all of the children's needs within the regular classroom program. One of the problems we had to solve was how much help to give children when they began their work.

The dilemmas I faced in working with Justin included how to enable him to have equal access to the curriculum and to build his ability to work on his own and with a partner. Because Justin would not start work on his own, especially any work on paper, adults were always watching him and jumping in to help him.

OBSERVATIONS LEAD TO ACTION

This became apparent one day when our school support teacher came to observe Justin working on math. He had been absent, and the lesson for the day was dependent on the work of the previous 2 days. So when I finished the first part of the math time, I made it a point to work for a few minutes with Justin to get him started. As soon as I thought he could continue on his own, I left him. Not 2 minutes went by before a student volunteer went over to Justin to see how he was doing. When she left him, Mrs. Liddy went over to check on him. Later, the support teacher said to me, "How can he work on his own with so many people checking in to help him?" Everyone was trying to "help" Justin. As a result, Justin did not have a chance to learn to work on his own. He was used to this level of support and attention and he knew that someone would come to his rescue. I began to think we were giving him the message that he couldn't begin work on his own in academic areas and we needed to change that message.

So, we, the adults in the class, sat down together and made a plan to leave Justin alone and to expect him to begin work on his own. If he needed help, he could ask for it, but we agreed to stop "hovering." Sometimes, well-meaning adults do that to children who appear to need a lot of help and children learn to depend on someone else to solve their problems for them. We talked directly to Justin about our plan and made it clear that we thought he could begin on his own.

At about the same time, I noticed that Justin often chose to draw during our class activity time. In order to further his participation in class discussions, I asked him if we could describe a piece of his work, and he agreed, somewhat sheepishly, but with interest, evidenced by a slow smile and a little sparkle in his eyes. I brought his drawing to the class meeting and asked each child to say something about it. We had done this before with other children's work and the students knew how to make descriptive, not evaluative, comments. We went around with every child making a statement. I wrote their descriptions on large chart paper, which was displayed later in the room. Up to this point, Justin's work had not been noticed or valued in the classroom. But once the children looked closely at his drawing and made statements about what they saw, it was clear that Justin was an artist and he was recognized and supported as an artist by me, Mrs. Liddy, and every child in the class.

As I reflected on this, I began to wonder whether Justin might invest more in his paper work if he could draw his responses to math problems and not get stuck on using words, which was still hard for him. I knew I would accept drawings for a response, but I didn't know if that was clear to Justin. I began to be explicit about how he could use drawing to convey what he knew in math.

Over the next few weeks, Justin combined drawing and math, using symbols and signs to convey his solutions and methods of solving problems. When he was part of a group of four children who were working on sorting data and making graphs, his visual and artistic skills were valued by the other members of the group. He had a place in the group, and he also began to have a place in the class. Children stopped by his table to watch him draw during activity time, and some began to copy his work or ask him to make a drawing for them. He produced visual work in response to class themes and curriculum in other content areas, such as science and social studies. He knew we expected him to write too, but being able to begin with the drawing and then move to writing allowed him to start from his strengths to show what he knew.

"A DIFFERENT PRESENCE"

One day in late January, a special education teacher in our school who had observed Justin in the classroom earlier in the year said to me, "What's happened with Justin? He has a different presence when he walks down the hall. He's not hanging his head down and ignoring people. He moves like a different person, someone who has confidence." Her comments at first were startling to me because when you are with a child day after day, change is gradual and you don't see it so sharply. I knew that Justin was much more responsive to the ideas and knowledge that were being developed in the classroom. But it sometimes takes an outsider to point out bigger changes.

I am committed to providing equity for all the students in my classroom. Each child must have the opportunity to grow as a thinker and a learner. I believe that entry points for diverse learners must be seen and recognized by the teachers and adults in the classroom. I have found that when each child's strengths, interests, and talents are noticed and validated by the important adults in the environment, the children become capable of taking the initiative to participate more actively in their own learning.

Evidence that this approach worked with Justin could be seen regularly by the spring. When it was time for the class to gather to share solutions and strategies for math problems, Justin would often ask me if he could stay at his table and work "a few more minutes" on his problem! He wanted to be sure that his solution on paper was clear and complete—a big change for a 2nd-grader who hadn't been able to begin paper-and-pencil work on his own in September.

The changes in Justin as a learner in our class were gradual. All the adults who worked or volunteered in the room took "small" actions based on their observations. We watched and thought about Justin, we noticed what he was good at, what he liked to do, his strengths. As a group jointly responsible for the learning of all the children in the class, we observed and described the impact of "hovering" adults, then sat down together and decided to get out of Justin's way. We communicated to him how he could get help when he needed it. We noticed his interest and skill in drawing and brought that forward using a process that involved each child and created a climate of respect for his strengths. We helped him learn how to begin his paper-and-pencil tasks with what he was good at—drawing—then encouraged him to add signs, symbols, labels, words, and sentences as he became more skillful. I like to think about "starting small," whether it's changing a classroom design, where inches often can make a difference in how space is utilized, or in taking one small observation of a child and acting on an idea based on that observation. Listening to the ideas of all the adults who know children and making small changes that emerge from discussing those ideas can have a big impact over time on a child's growth and learning.

PART V

Sustaining the Struggle

Vision and Vigilance

The teachers in this last section of the book, guided by visions of how schools could be, remain vigilant to school policies and educational directives that have visibly negative effects on children and teachers. They find ways to resist: to push the boundaries in order to make more space within the confines and to look for openings for action—alone or with others, surreptitiously or overtly. All of the authors tell of "small" changes made at the level of the classroom or school, and some also take political action at the local or national level. While these teachers may not always be successful, they remain hopeful and persistent, committed to sustaining the struggle to bring about change and to enacting their visions of humane and thoughtful education.

In "We Still Have Books, We Still Have Questions," Betsy Wice tells how the teachers at Frederick Douglass School in Philadelphia remain watchful for ways to keep alive the school's rich traditions of literacy, science, Black history, and questioning. The teachers' struggle to maintain a lively curriculum against the demands of rigid, scripted programs derives its strength from years of shared conversations and school projects. In "Wiggle Room," Chris Powers describes how he resists the limitations of the Philadelphia core curriculum by creating "wiggle room" for things he enjoys and that are meaningful to the children. Katharine Walmsley, in "Off and Running," tells how she meets some of the challenges of being a first-year teacher in an urban school with many children living in poverty. Even as a new teacher, she finds ways to deal with a required reading assessment so her students can be "left alone to do the real work of learning to read and write."

The first three chapters in Part V focus on taking action at the level of the classroom and school. Anne Martin's "Reclaiming Kindergarten" challenges us to pay attention to policies and trends, such as the use of checklists and standardized

135

tests, that threaten to transform kindergarten away from creativity, imaginative play, and authentic learning towards ever-narrowed concepts of childhood and learning. Her piece gives examples of resistance from teachers and parents, and is a call to broader political action.

CHAPTER 14

We Still Have Books, We Still Have Questions

Betsy Wice

I enter Esther Warren's room, on a warm June morning, to see if it's a good time for me to pull Marcus and Sam out into the hall for our reading group. Mrs. Warren has her whole 1st-grade class gathered around her on the rug. She is holding up a richly illustrated, new hardback book, *The Patchwork Path*. She reads aloud with animation and pleasure, stopping to discuss the pictures and to engage in questions. I spot Marcus on the edge of the group, totally absorbed. I'm not going to pull him out now, so I take a seat at the side of the room. "Why would a stormy night be a good time to escape?" Mrs. Warren asks.

"The masters would stay inside and wouldn't chase them," a girl volunteers. Marcus says, "Remember when we were reading the other book and he hid himself in a pretend casket?" Others chime in, "Oh, yeah!" Mrs. Warren affirms, "Yes, that was a way to escape, too. Isn't that clever?" Mrs. Warren reads on, coming to the phrase "scatter like flies." A student raises his hand, "You mean, they go in different directions?" There is a picture of the crossroads. Several hands go up to ask what that is. "Like an X? To decide which way to go?" "Like, which way to go in life?" Mrs. Warren remarks that they've raised a good point, that there are crossroads on a trip and there are crossroads in life. The classroom assistant, who has been eagerly leaning in toward the book, murmurs, "So true!"

A boy asks, "Why are they still trying to escape further, if they're already in Ohio and Ohio is free." Mrs. Warren briefly explains that Canada is another country, one without laws that require people to catch escaped slaves and bring them back to their masters.

The group moves on to discuss the distinction between Poppa and Hanna (escaped slaves) and others in the story who are free Black men. Marcus wonders, "Where is his sister? Is the book over?" Mrs. Warren flips back through the book. "We don't know if his sister got sold to another slave owner. You could get sold then, like a car." Then she finds the Afterword. "Bettye Stroud is telling us that this story is true, that she heard it from her great aunt." "So the author got the story from a slave?"

"Yes, a story could be told aloud, orally, passed down from one person to the next generation."

The Patchwork Path is not part of the official curriculum for grade 1 literacy at Douglass School. It is not teaching material from the kit distributed by Voyager Universal Literacy. Esther had spotted the book at our April book fair and bought it for her class. Somehow she has made time for it.

In another life Esther was a lawyer, increasingly discouraged by the justice system. If only she could work with these men and women at a younger age, before they ended up in trouble. Esther took advantage of the Literacy Intern program to make a career change. This was her second year as a classroom teacher assigned to 1st grade. The rigid pace and scripted lessons of Voyager Universal Literacy had not helped develop a calm and productive community of learners. Esther herself bridled at the Voyager training. At one Saturday workshop, she had asked the trainer, "What if the students have questions?"

The trainer said, "Don't allow for questions. It throws off the schedule." Esther and her 1st-grade colleagues adhered somewhat to the daily Voyager lessons and kept up with the Dynamic Indicators of Basic Early Literacy (DIBELS) assessments required by the district in compliance with No Child Left Behind (NCLB). But each teacher found time in the mandated literacy block for other interests. Esther brought horseshoe crab shells back from the New Jersey shore one Monday and excitedly described the spring mating and egg laying. In all three 1st-grade rooms, the children joined the school's annual silkworm project, avidly watching the tiny eggs hatch in mid-April. They were eager to help collect enough mulberry leaves to feed the ravenous appetites of the growing larvae. Many children brought in shoeboxes for raising extra silkworms at home. In May, the children watched with wonder as the silkworms spun their yellow silk cocoons. In June, the emerging moths held them spellbound with their vigorous mating and methodical egg laying. The more the children observed, the more questions they asked. We looked for answers in our crates of books about insects. Classrooms throughout the school took turns with the class set of *Silkworms* by Sylvia Johnson.

Meanwhile, in the official (mandated) science curriculum, a company named K12 Inc. mailed painted lady larvae kits to the 2nd grades. The tiny caterpillars and their prepackaged food arrived on April 7, just in time for the children to see them crawl around a bit before Easter vacation. The children returned from vacation 10 days later to discover a lot of dead butterflies. The classrooms had been empty while the caterpillars had made their chrysalises, emerged as butterflies, and flapped around a while in their net cages.

LEGACY OF BOOKS AND QUESTIONING

I was lucky to be sitting in on Esther's 1st-grade class that June morning when she was reading *The Patchwork Path*. The room had a familiar feel to it, a particular vibrancy that can happen when there are plenty of questions and plenty of books. It felt like the good old days, before No Child Left Behind.

Our school had a legacy of questioning and a legacy of books. It was built in 1938 as an annex to the crowded Singerly School. It was named for Frederick Douglass only after a public campaign led by Singerly's principal Arthur Huff Fauset. Fauset was a teacher, writer, and anthropologist who had decided to challenge the "Whites only" system for assigning principals to public schools. In 1926 he had scored so well on eligibility tests that his name moved to the top of the principals' list. He asked to be put in charge of the next available school. The Board of Education complied by sending him to Singerly and then removed every White child from the school to send them to other schools nearby. The Board resisted renaming the school after Frederick Douglass because he was "too militant" to be a role model. Fauset led neighborhood marches and protests to have the annex named for Douglass. The Board offered a compromise. The new name would be "Douglass-Singerly." During his 20 years as principal, Fauset insisted on a rigorous dual curriculum: regular studies and "Negro studies." There was no textbook for elementary children to study Black history, so Fauset wrote it. We still have copies of the handsome blue hardcover titled *For Freedom* (1927). *For Freedom* presents a series of biographies, from Phillis Wheatley and Crispus Attucks to Fauset's own contemporaries (and colleagues) in the Harlem Renaissance. "As seen through such lives, the Negro appears no longer a creature destined merely to be a hewer of wood and a drawer of water, but a factor in our nation who has a real gift to offer to the world" (Fauset, 1927, p. 79).

The old name Singerly disappeared. But Frederick Douglass continued to be honored—in more than name only—as we retold the story of one boy's struggle for literacy and freedom. Long after Fauset's era, a tradition persisted of going out of our way to make sure we had plenty of good books for the children. In the 1980s and 1990s, we pursued grants to build up a collection of what we called Whole Books for the Whole School. We continued to guard our collection—class sets of 30 or more copies of each title, eventually more than 350 titles, including *The Gingerbread Man, Tar Beach, Bony-Legs, Tikki Tikki Tembo, Roll of Thunder Hear My Cry, Silkworms, Hatchet,* and *Narrative of the Life of Frederick Douglass*.

In 2001, several administrators, sent to help us make Adequate Yearly Progress, tried to get rid of what they perceived to be "clutter." We were told to bring down to the Dumpster any books not in the standardized curriculum. Luckily, the Whole Books for the Whole School collection was housed at the back of Doris Rearden's custodial closet. She kept them safe.

Doris Rearden's book closet continued to delight new teachers at Douglass, though we didn't get to use the class sets as much as we had before No Child Left Behind. Still, Gail Connelly found time to read Karen Hesse's *Out of the Dust* with her 8th-graders. (Gail reported to me that many of them cried, including her.) Most of the 2nd-, 3rd-, and 4th-grade classes continued the 4-H embryology project, with Selsam's *Egg to Chick* as their text. (When Toni James's chicks failed to hatch, we got out the set of Johnson's *Inside an Egg* to guide our autopsies of the embryos. We estimated that the unborn chicks had died between Day 13 and Day 15.)

Down the hall, Molly Rand and Karen Ward had each begun to realize that their special education classes were under less surveillance for following the mandated curriculum. Molly's students read their way through the collection of Horrible Harry and Song Lee books, the Angela Shelf Medearis mysteries, and many of the Magic Tree House titles. Karen and her students became enthralled with classical mythology, especially the *Adventures of Hercules* and *D'Aulaire's Book of Greek Myths*.

Like the 1st grades, the 2nd-grade classes were saddled with Voyager Universal Literacy and its insipid phonics-based stories. At the end of October, their story concerned two phonically named children on a camping trip in their own backyard. The vocabulary words included *compass, flashlight, campfire*. Erin Scott was getting tired of the blank looks she was receiving when she delivered the scripted lesson, so she worked with the children to write invitations to a camping trip that would take place in Room 209. The children's parents and also Douglass colleagues received the handmade invitations. The evening before the "trip," Erin and her husband set up a very large tent in Room 209. As the children entered the next morning, they took their places in a circle inside the tent, in front of a cardboard "fire" they had constructed. Erin excused herself and soon reentered with a walking stick and a spelunking helmet. I scooted into the tent at 9:15, with a compass. We passed it around and conversed about N, S, E, W. The talk turned to speculations about how you would find north if you didn't have a compass. The room was dark, except for the glow of the flashlight-lit fire. The mood was magical. We started to sing "Follow the Drinking Gourd" (but not very well). Our computer teacher, Bob Mooney, was just entering. He excused himself and returned with his laptop and a disk that played Kim and Reggie Harris's spirited rendition. We talked more about the codes for escaping and about Peg Leg Joe. Erin's student teacher,

Diane Davey, wondered about the quilt codes. The next day she pulled me aside and asked me where all that information could be found. She had never heard about the Drinking Gourd and the North Star and the songs' double meanings. She borrowed class sets *of Sweet Clara and the Freedom Quilt, Young Harriet Tubman,* and *Barefoot: Escape on the Underground Railroad.* Erin and Diane found time to build on the students' interest in that history. They skimped on some of the Voyager activities to give the children chances to dramatize what they had read together and to write and illustrate their own escape stories.

A few days later, Erin and Diane planned a map lesson for a neighborhood walk that took the children past Pearl Bailey's house, only a block away— Pearl Bailey went to our school! They used the compass to navigate their way around the nearby blocks, taking snapshots of murals and historical markers.

WE STILL HAVE BOOKS

The Whole Books collection continued to grow even as NCLB mandates became more restrictive. We continued to encourage the generosity of outside friends, who paid for new sets of books. The new 6th-grade science teacher wanted *War of the Worlds* to enrich his unit on space. We ordered a set. The children loved it. The new 6th-grade English teacher requested *Journey to Jo'burg.* Their shared reading blossomed into projects in art and in writing that went far beyond the required lessons. Gail Connelly wanted to try *The House on Mango Street,* which led to an outpouring of student poetry, which in turn sparked a new tradition of open mic nights. When I retired as reading specialist/literacy leader, the books and the silkworms and the chick eggs continued to provide me with daily entry into Douglass classrooms.

Our last Douglass Book Fair was in 2010. Under the "Renaissance" initiative, our school district dispersed the Frederick Douglass staff and handed over the school to Scholar Academies, a private management company. We gathered up copies of *For Freedom* and other Douglass School artifacts to deposit into the Urban Archives at Temple University. We marshaled vans and station wagons to carry books to classrooms around the city where our teachers were reassigned.

We former Douglass teachers stay in touch. As a retired volunteer I get around to several of my colleagues' current classrooms. We continue to share books with each other and with the children. Each spring we gather mulberry leaves for a new generation of silkworms. In June 2013, when the school district closed 23 neighborhood public schools, teachers alerted us about more abandoned book closets and libraries. Again, we mobilized to load up cartons of books for surviving classrooms.

CHAPTER 15

Wiggle Room

Pushing the Boundaries

Chris Powers
(In conversation with Betsy Wice)

Chris Powers teaches grade 3 at the Samuel Powel Elementary School, a public school in West Philadelphia. His older daughter, Sofia, is in kindergarten at Powel, and the two of them walk the few blocks to school together each morning. Chris and Betsy met 4 years prior to this conversation, when he arrived in Philadelphia as a new teacher at her school, Frederick Douglass, in North Philadelphia. He taught there for 2 years, teaching grade 6 and then grade 3.

Betsy: I was the reading teacher at Douglass and enjoyed collaborating with Chris. Though we missed him when he left Douglass, we were pleased he could continue his work in his own neighborhood school, a small K–4 school that has managed to keep education lively for its diverse student body. We've stayed in touch through our local inquiry group, the Philadelphia Teachers Learning Cooperative.

When I sat down to talk with Chris, he was sporting the beginnings of a beard. He explained that he'd been out sick for a few days the week before. Rather than shave before returning to school, he had decided to let the beard grow until after the state exams (PSSA) later in the month. I asked him what it was like for him this year, teaching at Powel.

Chris: Just to start, I can say some of the difficulties of trying to do it. With the core curriculum and the Benchmark testing and now with the PSSA testing, I'm finding that some of the things I value in teaching or enjoy doing more are not the core of my teaching. They're supplementary.

I guess times have changed. I'm still trying to do a lot of the things I value, but the pacing schedule we're given is so intense. If you were to follow it by the book, it doesn't allow for very much wiggle room at all.

There are some genuinely good things. This core curriculum is a halfway decent framework for things that 3rd-graders should know by the end of the year. We've now been told if we can cover it with our own materials, then go ahead, as long as it's being covered. But the pacing and timing is very intense. In 3rd grade, every 6 weeks we're given the Benchmark Assessment, not only the literacy and math but also the science benchmarks. Those are the city-mandated tests. A lot of that is making sure that you know the wording of what was in the textbooks. So, sometimes children truly get the concept, and then they're asked one of these questions that's just worded a little differently. Some of the kids are able to process what they've learned and think through that, but overall, it's almost a vocabulary test: "What was the actual wording in the book?"

Betsy: So do you find yourself taking your stuff and matching it to the vocabulary?

Chris: Trying to. I'd love to be able to say that I don't care and I can throw this all out and we're going to do all meaningful things, but then I would find that the kids themselves would be devastated taking these tests and feeling as though they were failures. Our school has its data wall that is now mandated by our regional superintendent. That data from the Benchmarks has to be on a prominent bulletin board as you walk in the front door. It is something that's out there—even though the Benchmark Assessments are technically for me to assess how I'm teaching and what the students are getting. The school district comes back with all of your results, with these lovely documents saying, "Your school didn't do well on this, this, and this. Here are some strategies you can use." We spend half of our grade group meetings discussing the results. I can't say that the discussion of it is not helpful. The best piece of that talk is seeing where the children have made some errors and why they made them. A lot of it is simply the test-taking skills and the wording.

Those are the pieces I feel locked into, as well as the PSSA test, which this year is even earlier than last year. So some of the things that we cover later in the year—we still have 3 months left in the year— are prominent items on this PSSA test. We've been in a crash course here on a few things, getting the basics, and then we'll go back and investigate them later.

At Powel we do the math curriculum called Investigations. It really allows for investigation and exploration. It's something that I enjoy following because it actually does allow wiggle room. There are lots of manipulatives, lots of exploring, lots of finding your own meaning.

OPENINGS

Betsy: Can you tell me about something in math that worked well?

Chris: We just started in on fractions. That's something they really enjoyed last year, and I'm seeing the same enthusiasm this year. A lot of it is the hands-on piece, lots of pattern blocks, with things that they have discovered throughout the years since kindergarten—which pieces fit together neatly and which don't. Now they're all of a sudden taking these concepts and being able to put names and numbers to them. You can see that they really enjoy figuring this out, making the connections between these pattern blocks. Or we talk about sharing brownies. At this point they're paper brownies, but eventually we will go to sharing real brownies and real food. It's something that, now that they have that connection, we can talk about on a daily basis, even if it's "five-sixths of this table is ready." We recently had someone bring in pudding cups. They were chocolate and vanilla. We were able to connect that—what fraction was chocolate.

They're also enjoying something we've been making from the multiplication and division unit. We now have four Riddle Books in our classroom. They're all story problems written by the students. We started with this basic pattern: "There are 5 oranges in a box. Johnny went and bought 6 boxes of oranges. How many oranges did he have all together?" That's the basic format but some of the kids have taken it into elaborate stories. Some kids got stuck on aliens and space ships. They went beyond the basic format: "There are 5 aliens in a spaceship and there are 10 spaceships." Now there's a whole story that goes behind that. The math problem is woven into a very creative story.

Then there's lots of illustrating they get to do, because part of the Investigations curriculum is using not only numbers but also words and pictures to describe the process that they're going through in math. We talk about efficiency in pictures, but these riddle books have allowed them something different. This is where you don't have to just draw a circle and four legs, you don't have to be efficient; this is some place where you can stretch a little bit.

Betsy: How much time do they have to work on the Riddle Stories?

Chris: It's part of our math time. I'm supposed to be doing 90 minutes a day of math, so they had a good 35 to 40 minutes doing the riddle book each day.

Betsy: So if you're a kid getting involved in your picture, you're not going to get cut short.

Chris: Or, there will be time, you're going to finish it tomorrow. You can expand on it. Some of the kids who really like to expand are the ones who were struggling with math a little, but art is their thing. They still have the time to expand. Also, that work on your riddle story is a great thing to do when you're done with something else at another time of the day. At some point we do need to move on. I will make sure that they have one piece completed. But it's something that some of them have even gone back and done on their own time.

Betsy: Do you keep the Riddle Books in the classroom?

Chris: They're in three-ring binders. Some of them are a couple of months old. They're pretty worn and tattered looking because the kids go into them a lot. Other books we have in the class, ones that I've noticed they've gone back into, are the Current Events books. Part of the homework has been Current Events, where I ask them to simply go into a newspaper, magazine, anything that they want, and pick out some type of article and do a who-what-when-where-why summary of it, one a week. I've also been keeping those in a binder. The kids just recently discovered last year's binder in a little corner in the library area.

The Current Events homework is fun for them. I'm getting a lot of magazine celebrity cutouts, music stars, tiny articles, almost captions—you'll find a lot of their background knowledge. Last year I had a few parents who said, "This article isn't appropriate," but I stress that this is their kid's choice. Some of the parents are pushing them to read something more. That's good. I'll ask the kid to do two a week, let them have fun with one of them.

Betsy: Homework, math, as places for wiggle room. What else?

THE LEARNING GARDEN

Chris: What I'm looking forward to soon is a tree observation project, as the seasons change. They choose a tree or plant that they have access to every day. I'll be asking them to do drawing, writing, and observations. It even gets into some point-of-view writing—the point of view of the tree: who's walking by, what's happening. We'll do some writing every day. Where do *they* see it from every day? Just now, we're watching the changes that are occurring in the trees. We've had the chance to talk about seeing the buds pop up. I've discovered now that our yard, these little few houses here, must be on some robins' migratory AAA maps. This is the third year in a row where I've experienced it, that we'll walk out and see upwards of 200 robins, on every ledge, every roof, every tree. They strip our holly tree clean of berries. And our neighbor has an enormous holly. The robins will be here for an hour or two, big fat robins. We talked about that in class, and that got us into spring, noticing some of the changes.

Betsy: Is there something in the curriculum that nods toward that?

Chris: Thankfully, for me, plants/life cycle is the rest of our year's science. That's where I will find all my wiggle room—just because it is my personal love. We'll spend a lot of time out in the garden that we have at Powel. Last year was the first full year with a garden back there in the playground. My daughter's kindergarten class has spent some time there, too. Last fall my class went with Sofia's class and planted bulbs out there—probably over 100 daffodils, tulips, I don't even know (somebody handed me a large bag of bulbs). That's a place, fortunately, that falls within the 3rd-grade curriculum. At our staff meeting yesterday I requested a show of hands of who wants to use the garden. We designed it so that there would be at least one 4-by-8 raised bed for each classroom. Last year my class and one other class were the only ones to do anything in it. It was brand new at that point. This year, it looks like we'll be about four—myself and three other teachers—maybe five. It's the Learning Garden. That's what we call it.

Betsy: So no one's going to get in trouble for being out in the Learning Garden?

Chris: No. It's a place where you can obviously tie in all kinds of writing, all kinds of math. Even if you're not someone who wants to get your class digging in the garden, it's there. There's no reason that you can't observe and talk about it and measure. If you didn't plant that tomato and my class did, it's perfectly fine that you go out there and measure it.

I'd love to set up a Learning Garden binder. When I was interning in New Hampshire, we designed a whole curriculum map around maple sugaring. If I could take that same concept and use it in the garden—here's "The Learning Garden" in the middle and here are the endless possibilities of how you can squeeze this into your curriculum. You can teach verbs and nouns off of it if you really want. You can stretch this as far as you like. That's a plan that's in the back of my mind, along with everything else.

GOING DEEPER

Talking about the future—I'm hoping for one without budget cuts so I can maintain my position here at Powel. I'm hoping I can stick here and in this grade and be familiar enough with the core curriculum and the pacing schedule and take some summer time to figure out how I can do what they're asking me to do. Take the concepts of what they're asking me to do and almost design my own curriculum around it. Obviously a very flexible one, too, because even in the few years that I've been doing this, I have rarely had something work the same the second time around. I actually started the spring tree-watching project with the 3rd-graders at Douglass, on a smaller scale. I was supposed to be teaching the plant life cycle in 3rd grade there, too, which took us in a different direction—for many of the children just to realize that there were trees right on their block. It wasn't as tree-filled an area as this is. I would hear the first day, "No, there isn't one, I can't find a tree anywhere. There is no tree." So we talked about the ones right outside the building. This tree can be one that every day when you walk outside you can look at it for 5 minutes. We took a walk around the Douglass School and did bark rubbings and looked at even some of the very hardy and bizarre weeds that were growing in certain areas, just showing them, there is life there. I don't even know the names of those elephant-ear plants that grow up.

When you look at this core curriculum guide, there are standards that pop up every week. "Acquiring New Vocabulary"—very general things. That's something that I want to look into. How can I take that and go deeper? There's almost too much to do if you were to just follow what you're supposed to do. I can't stand just doing that. I've got all these other ideas and I'm trying to piece them in. Things do get cut out of my ideas; things do get cut out of the core curriculum. Unfortunately on occasion I have to go back and say, "OK, you need to be exposed to . . ." I get a chance to look at these 6-week Benchmark tests a day or two early and say, "Now I feel bad that we missed that because there are three questions on here, so yes, it is something important." We talk about it: "This is a game and how can you play this game and do well at it, so that we can move on to the other games."

WIGGLE ROOM AND RESISTANCE

Betsy: I like the way you're growing a beard from now until after the tests, the game idea. What basketball coaches do . . .

Chris: One of my smallest children came over, "I'm not shavin' either!" I liked that. I was out 2 days sick, then when I came in last week, they said, "Something's different." It's just one way to make light of the testing.

Recently I went out for lunch with a colleague, Gill, and some doctoral students from Penn. One of the Penn students had an idea of taking the ScanTron sheets and doing watercolors over them. We talked about making them into impressionistic paintings, taking different colors and filling in the dots, that's just a way of demystifying these instruments. Almost civil disobedience.

Betsy: That fits in with some of these other things: the garden, the math Riddle Books, the Current Events books. An aesthetic side to classroom work.

Chris: Something that's real world. No Child Left Behind is kind of cramping everybody. If you went into teaching for the art of teaching, the love of teaching, it's squeezing that out a little. If you had wanted to take the

children, who they are, their outside lives, and bring that into the school.
. . . Now all of these mandates, testing things, seem to be pushing all of
that outside, keeping that outside. Sometimes all that gets brought into
the school is the negative pieces of what's outside the school.

My daughter is a kindergartner. No Child Left Behind has taken
a lot of the play out. It's taking away social interaction and learning.
Thankfully Sofia's kindergarten teacher can say, "I've been doing this
long enough, and I can't change for you like this. We're still going
to play. Yes, I'll get to all of that stuff, and yes, I need to because I
know that you 1st-, 2nd-, 3rd-, and 4th-grade teachers are expected
to jump right in on this level and the children are expected to have
this information, so we will get there." I think for society as a whole,
it's going to take a toll, when society is not valuing investigation,
play, and learning through play, which is the most developmentally
appropriate way to figure out about the world.

Betsy: Powel School is going to work for Sofia, the next couple of years?

Chris: Sofia soaks up everything. At Powel you have a range of ethnic and
socioeconomic backgrounds. That's what we enjoy about it, too. This
is real life. We chose to live in the city, here. These are all of the people
you will see in your life. We're all in this together. We enjoy that. I feel
comfortable with Sofia at Powel. We walk to school, and then I see her
two or three times a day. I pop into her kindergarten classroom while
they're doing journal writing every day. This teacher has not given that
up. It's set to the individual child. There are different goals that she's
working on with each child. They really get to draw. That's a place
where they get to bring in their life, things they're interested in.

Powel School has a history of finding the wiggle room, wherever
it was. There have been projects for years: the Biography Project,
the African, Greek, or Chinese culture projects, which are part of a
schoolwide thematic unit every spring. It's still there. There was a big
discussion in yesterday's staff meeting, how so much is chopped up by
the testing schedule. But we've had the Biography Project, and we're
still hanging on to the thematic unit. Last year was China. We used
the garden to make an abstract Chinese dragon with red and yellow
flowers. This year it's Greece. I'd like to take that into the garden, too.

Now we've got the Emerging Scholars program again. Last year it
turned into a management piece to overcome, to set up interest groups
for teachers and students. Here you are with a whole new batch of
students for 2 hours, one day a week. It was difficult, but for some of
us, "If the district is going to tell me that I have 2 hours to do anything
that I love to do, please, I'll gladly take it. Hey, they're giving us the
money, let's do it the way we can." We teachers each displayed on the
bulletin board what our interests were, and the kids chose, based on a

little two-sentence summary of what we thought we were going to do. Some of us took it as, "Here's my interest, let's find out what the kids like, let's make it really student centered." Others went into it saying, "I have 8 weeks of plans down to the minute, here's what we'll do." They each had their place.

Betsy: So you're always looking for ways to bring in things that are really important to the kids, work that is real to them.

Chris: We're trying to do that more with writing, too. That's my tough spot. I've been trying—and my colleague Gill has been helping a lot—to make persuasive writing meaningful by thinking of something they would really like to persuade people about. Last year I took some of my students to the School Reform Commission meeting. During all the budget cuts, some of my students actually presented their persuasive writing to the commission. This year, I've shared with the class a letter that my wife, Sonya, and I wrote for the upcoming budget hearings. It was a piece of persuasive writing: Here's Powel School. We can't have another cut. Here are all the wonderful things we do.

Wearing my three hats as parent, teacher, community member, I end up at more meetings than I care to ever . . . home and school, school council, the School Reform Commission. . . .

Betsy: It puts you right at the throbbing center of all this. I thought our conversation would be about just the classroom. But it has to be more than that.

Chris: I have to make it more than my classroom. This is my neighborhood I chose to live in. This is my child's school. Sometimes I almost wish I could forget all about the rest of it, spend more time with just my classroom stuff, but I can't escape all of this. In spite of all the pressures from above I am committed to working to sustain Powel's history of making space for investigations that have real meaning for children and teachers. It's what makes teaching and learning so gratifying.

CHAPTER 16

Off and Running

Pushing Back and Creating Community

Katharine Walmsley

I began my teaching career right in the middle of things. I had finished grad-uate school a few weeks earlier and had enjoyed a successful and satisfying internship that fall in a 3rd grade in a rural town in Massachusetts. But I had very little experience working in urban settings and was well aware that I was really getting in over my head.

Nonetheless, in I went.

The teacher I took over for had left in the middle of the year because of urgent family business. I spent much of the year just trying to create a safe classroom climate. I had students who were screaming, fighting, and locking themselves in the closet, and I even had a student light a fire in the bathroom. Although I was not able to truly build a classroom community or even fully gain control of the class, I went ahead with some of the curricula and ideas that were important to me. I taught songs and dances. I read aloud and provided good literature for kids to read. I did science. We wrote books together. Many kids—including those whose behavior was problematic—re-sponded to these activities. Those first few months of teaching were, on the whole, much more difficult than rewarding.

A lot of things changed in my first full year of teaching. Although I did start at the beginning of the year, I only found out that I was teaching 1st grade a few days before the school year began. There was a new principal and a lot of changes within the building. The entire student population shifted in a district-wide return to neighborhood schools. Only four students from my class the previous year returned to the school.

I work in a K–5 urban elementary school of about 300 students. About 72 percent of the children receive free or reduced-price lunch. About 50 per-cent of children in the district do not speak English as their first language.

The vast majority of these English language learners (ELL) are native Spanish speakers. My own classes have had a particularly high concentration of beginner and intermediate ELL students. These students were placed in the same class so they could receive some support from an ELL teacher and also because I am the only person at my grade level who speaks Spanish.

I went into the classroom with a lot of ideas and values about what the classroom and curriculum should look like, but it quickly became apparent that there was no way to get things to be as good as I wanted as soon as I wanted. Instead, I chose some things to implement that I thought of as nonnegotiable, others that I wanted to implement as soon as possible, and a few that I let go of right at the start, knowing that within a few years I would be ready to take them on. The nonnegotiable things were those I considered most important and also those that simply made me the happiest to share with children.

CLASSROOM AS COMMUNITY

On the first day of school I was struck by how many students were delivered to my door by one or more of their parents or grandparents. The previous year I had had a lot of difficulty connecting with or even getting in touch with parents. I was happy to be able to start the year off connecting with the parents and inviting them to stay in touch and be involved.

The children and I spent the next couple of weeks getting to know each other and establishing the classroom routines. I took the time to take the class outside to play games, to teach and practice routines and ways to use classroom materials, and to teach the class a range of songs from very silly songs—beautiful, slow songs; and songs in Spanish to quite a few with movements or dances. The previous year I had encountered some resistance to learning songs and dances from kids who felt like it wasn't "cool." But my class this year was appropriately "immature" and it felt a lot more like I had anticipated teaching 1st grade would be. The songs were received with absolute delight and enthusiasm. The students kept notebooks with a copy of each song or poem we learned in which they illustrated the pages. These notebooks were one of the things students chose to show their parents at Back-to-School Night, and many parents commented on how much they and their children were enjoying the songs.

The single most important idea I brought into teaching was the importance of a child feeling emotionally, socially, and physically safe. Children need to feel known in order to succeed in school. They needed to know that I cared about them and what was going on in their lives both in and out of school. They also needed to understand that I expected them to treat each other well and that I would not accept otherwise. That is nonnegotiable for me. I tried to lay the groundwork for a positive classroom environment through establishing not only rules but also routines from the very beginning of the year in order to create a shared knowledge and experience for our class to draw upon throughout the year.

Our day, for example, always started off with a morning meeting. This may be common in some schools, but it is the exception, not the rule, in mine. The meeting started off with a greeting. I remember those first few weeks of school when I had some students who couldn't even look at the persons next to them, let alone find a voice to greet them. Eventually the greetings started to flow easily without any prompting from me.

In January, a new student entered our class. Ricardo was shy, his English was limited, and he did not easily engage with other students. For weeks he refused to join us in the circle, pacing around the room and sometimes even bolting out the door. We, as a class, drew him into our morning greeting. Eventually we got Ricardo to sit with us in the circle, though he was looking down the entire time. By the last month of school he was able to participate in the greeting happily. The entire class had became invested in getting him to join the circle; it wasn't something I could have done on my own.

When I took this job, many of the teachers told me how uninvolved and apathetic parents of our students were about their children's progress in school. However, through newsletters home, phone calls, and talking to parents when they dropped off or picked up their children, I started to develop good working relationships with many parents during that first year. The fact that I speak Spanish was a real benefit for me with the parents who spoke only Spanish or whose English was limited. During my first set of parent conferences, one of my students came in with her three older sisters, her mother, her uncle, and her grandmother. The sisters were used to translating for their mother. When I spoke to her in my less-than-perfect Spanish, my student, the youngest in her family, lit up. It was a powerful connection for the child to see that her family and her teacher were willing to use languages that they were not completely comfortable with to talk about her and the progress she was making. I have found that when I am willing to speak in Spanish, parents are also more willing to try to speak to me in English. A space can be made somewhere in between the two languages for the important work of supporting a child in his or her growth and learning.

READING AND WRITING TOGETHER

Not long after I began teaching, my entire district was given a "turnaround partner" by the state of Massachusetts. The turnaround partner is a company that provides curriculum and support in a model designed to increase student performance. Ironically, the curriculum has almost no focus on teaching children to read and write.

In kindergarten, where children would typically become acquainted with stories, books, and print, more and more time is spent instead coaching children on discrete tasks that lead to higher scores on the required assessment. These same children are then expected to leave 1st grade as proficient readers. I constantly feel the pressure of these tests, of a curriculum that is not always reasonable, and of the expectation that the children will leave 1st grade as readers. Wherever possible I try to shield my students from that pressure. Instead of the abstract lessons suggested by the turnaround partner, I use a variety of strategies and activities that draw children into reading. I have also created space for my students to participate in small groups, to choose and read books independently, and to spend some time responding to literature in ways that are meaningful for them. I want my students to develop a love and understanding of books and stories, and at the same time learn the "mechanics" of reading.

In my first year I found some Reader's Theater plays in the literacy closet and helped some students who were already reading to put together performances for the rest of the class. The following year I wanted each student in the class to participate in a Reader's Theater performance. I started earlier in the year with some of the kids who could read, and they put on a performance of *Goldilocks and the Three Bears*. I invited a few people from around the school: the counselor, a child's grandmother who worked in the office, and a reading specialist who worked with our class. The children got such great feedback from having other adults there that I decided to start inviting parents to the performances. The second play of the year was *Sly Fox and the Little Red Hen*, performed by a group of four boys. I couldn't have been more pleased when all four of their fathers showed up for the play. Three of their mothers came as well. I have a great image of two of the fathers, who were easily more than 6 feet tall, sitting in tiny 1st-grade chairs, proudly watching their sons as the fox and the narrator.

The third play of the year was the *Three Billy Goats Gruff*, and it was a tough performance to pull off. The children in this group were beginning readers and the group included a girl named Grace, who was, at that point, in her fifteenth foster home since the age of 5. She struggled throughout the year with severe emotional challenges, eventually ending up in residential care. I had cast her as the eldest Billy goat sister (the goats were all girls and they decided that they would be sisters and not brothers), and we had worked extensively in the group to practice reading the lines and to create scenery. The day before the play, Grace had a visit with her biological mother and an appointment with a psychologist that had led to a decision to take her out of her foster home yet again and place her in another one that night. Although she was understandably upset, on this day she wanted more than anything to be in that play. She shone in the play. After the performance, I allowed each cast member to take a comment or question from an audience member, and Grace beamed as a classmate told her that his favorite part was when she pushed the troll at the end and he fell over.

I have found these plays to be a big source of excitement for all of my students, from the most fluent readers to the ones who are just beginning to read. The plays are about more than practicing reading. They have provided opportunities for students to draw on other strengths. After the performances the students continue to take the books from the classroom library and put on the plays during choice time. These plays create a space for the children to be invested in the class community.

Another vehicle for fostering a sense of community is writing workshop. All children have stories to tell. I encourage my students to write stories from their own lives. When Michelle started 1st grade her writing consisted of one or two sounds for each word, with the letters all strung together. Slowly, she began to put spaces between her words and, even more slowly, vowels started to appear. Reading was hard for her, but she was very eager to tell stories in writing and read them back to herself. About halfway through the year she worked on several stories about some difficult times her family had gone through. Later in the year she frequently wrote fiction stories about her family. When children feel safe in the classroom, they are usually willing to take the risk of sharing their writing with the class, and this becomes a powerful way for them to learn about each others' lives and interests.

"SHOULD I SKIP THE PERIODS?"

Early in my first full year of teaching all of my students were subjected to a round of Dynamic Indicators of Basic Early Literacy Skills (DIBELS) testing. DIBELS is used in my district to assess prereading and decoding skills. The new principal was very focused on phonics skills and put a huge emphasis on raising DIBELS scores.

During this first round of "DIBELing" I found out that my class's scores were very low. In fact, almost all of my class was below where kids are supposed to be when entering 1st grade. This was not surprising considering that I had most of the 1st-grade ELL students and several students with autism. In the beginning I wasn't concerned about the scores, primarily because I didn't think DIBELS was a very informative assessment. I put the scores in a folder and didn't think about them, or the assessment, until a few months later at a grade-level meeting with the principal at which we discussed the results of DIBELS "progress monitoring" that had taken place 6 weeks into the school year. In general, the scores from the classroom that had two full-time teachers, one of whom devoted the entire morning to drilling children in phonics, were a little higher than those of my class and the other 1st grade. The principal requested that those of us who were not specifically targeting the skills on the test begin to do so directly.

Of all the tasks in DIBELS, the one I struggle with the most is "nonsense word fluency." This task requires students to tell the sounds of individual letters grouped in twos or threes and, if possible, blend them into a nonsense word. It is particularly difficult for ELL students who don't yet have a grasp of the real words in English to be bombarded with nonsense words. I find that the less command of the English language students have, the more they try to make sense of nonsense words. Trying to make sense of the words takes up their time and leads to a lower score.

I talked to the children about what happens when we see nonsense words in real books such as those by Dr. Seuss and what we do to figure them out. Then we practiced a few times sounding out nonsense words quickly and reading them aloud. I told them that for this task all of the vowels would be short. When they took the test again in the spring, their scores were very high.

In the middle of the year and at the end of it a reading-fluency component is added to the DIBELS assessment. Students are asked to read as many words as possible from a passage in 1 minute. There is no comprehension component: Students are simply given a score based on how many words they are able to decode correctly. While I agree that students need to be proficient in oral reading fluency, I think this method is a very limited way of testing it. I was practicing with Isabella, a student who was a fairly fluent reader. We had read the first two passages, and I reminded her that when she did this task for the test (to be given the next week), she should go as fast as possible. She looked at me and asked very seriously, "Should I skip the periods?" I told her that for this task, and this task only, yes, she should plow right through the periods and just read as fast as she could.

Because the DIBELS focuses on fluency but not comprehension, a child's score can be misleading. Henry was a child who entered 1st grade speaking little English. He made incredible progress, and by the end of the year he had about the same score as children whose overall reading skills were significantly higher than his. Though he had become a strong decoder, his comprehension was still greatly affected by his limited English. He could not truly understand books at the level that his DIBELS score suggested, because he needed time to build his vocabulary and language skills in English.

The DIBELS assessment doesn't give me much information that I don't already have from spending 6 hours a day with my students reading, writing, speaking, doing math, singing, and working on science experiments. It doesn't give me any information that I can't get from the formal and informal assessments I am doing with students all the time. The compromise I've reached is to spend a little time reviewing the skills specifically and giving my students knowledge of how the test works so that they can perform as well as possible. The better I can get them to do, the more we are all left alone to do the real work of learning to read and write.

SCIENCE EXPLORATIONS

My undergraduate degree is in environmental studies, and before I became a teacher I worked as an environmental educator on the Clearwater, a tall ship that primarily offers "educational sails" with groups of schoolchildren. I am comfortable and experienced in doing science with children. Science, I have found out, is not the highest priority in my school district. At one point I was told by the principal that if I had to cut out science to get in more reading that would be all right with her. It would, however, be out of the question for me.

I decided to become a public school teacher because I loved teaching kids about the Hudson River when they came out on their class trips. I couldn't help but think of the impact I could have by taking one group of children on a year-long learning trip, as opposed to taking endless groups of children on 3-hour trips.

When I first took the job I was able to take my pick of the Full Option Science System (FOSS) kits for 1st grade. It seemed (and turned out to be true) that no one was really using them. I used some lessons and materials from the FOSS kits and supplemented them with my own ideas and projects. At times, it was difficult for me when I realized that what I was doing was nothing compared to the well-planned-and-executed unit on trees I had developed and taught during my internship. However, what my lessons may have lacked in polish didn't really matter to my students. On Back-to School Night they couldn't wait to show their parents the chrysalises that they had been watching every day for signs of change. Students who generally had a hard time writing were suddenly eager to make observations in their science journals about butterflies or weather experiments.

During an investigation into plants and the plant life cycle we grew tiny "lawns" in little plastic cups. Students were able to choose just how much grass and weed seeds to plant in their lawns. Then, as the lawns grew, they were able to "mow" their little lawns with scissors. No one in the class predicted that the lawns would grow back when we cut them. The class could hardly believe it when they came in on a Monday morning to find that their lawns had grown tall once again. When the children took their lawns home, a few of them decided to plant their lawns by their houses. Most of the children lived in apartments or other buildings with little or no outdoor space.

Still, they kept those little lawns alive, watering and cutting them at home for as long as they could. For weeks, I got reports from children about how their lawns were faring at home.

LOOKING BACK

When I look back on my first few years of teaching, I have a lot to be proud of. All of the kids I've taught have made progress academically, socially, and emotionally. Most of them left 1st grade as good readers, and those who were not solid readers yet left with a love of books and stories and a desire to keep working on their skills. Although I know that I have created space for many children to learn and feel known in the classroom, at times it has been a struggle to keep that space. All of the mandates coming at the national, state, district, and school levels exert daily pressure on me and, consequently, on my students. There are days when everything I have tried to put in place to help my students succeed is not enough to negate the fact that many of them come in hungry, tired, with shoes and clothes that don't fit, and bearing the scars of poverty.

I cannot change the reality of the children's lives. However, I can have a profound effect on their learning and their ability to find the confidence to see themselves as learners. Sometimes that has to be enough. As my skills and experience as a teacher expand, my confidence and ability to create space for my students to learn and to grow as individuals increases. I am learning every year and with each child I teach how to push back at the boundaries of the mandates to do what is right to help my students. While some things about who I am as a teacher have changed as I have gained experience, I still believe that the most important space that can be created in classrooms is for children to be known.

CHAPTER 17

Reclaiming Kindergarten

Anne C. Martin

> We took out a long sheet of paper that looked like an application for a mortgage. It had so many small squares, check marks, pluses and Xs, that we thought we would need a Guide for the Perplexed. Today's modern report cards are neither reports nor cards. . . . I looked at Katy's New Age report, which is now called the Academic Social Growth and Effort Indicator—TASGEI, for short—and counted 54 attributes subsumed under a variety of curriculum areas. For each area the students are ranked on a scale of 1 to 5, with 1 being the best. (Leon Schuchman, as cited in Shanker, 1995)

In 1995, when Katy's grandparent said this, checklist reports of primary school students were still somewhat of a novelty; they are now the norm. With standardized testing, benchmarks, and mandated curricula, school systems seem to be outdoing each other in creating and adopting so-called standards-based reports for kindergarten children as well as older students. The numbers of items to be checked off have mushroomed (often more than 70 on each report) and the rankings reinforce the emphasis on standards, for example:

- rarely meets standard
- sometimes meets standard
- usually meets standard
- consistently exceeds standard

Broad categories like social skills (sometimes termed life skills), language arts, mathematics, problem solving, science, social studies, fine and gross motor skills, and in some cases music and art are subdivided into minute parts. The forms vary in the detail of items to be evaluated, from a kindergarten report going so far as to include a list of the whole alphabet to check off in five columns, to reports that ask only whether the child recognizes and names all upper- and most lowercase letters.

In some reports, there are small blank spaces for teachers to add written comments. In order to soften the cold, impersonal language of the items and make them more "parent friendly," some reports couch the comments in the first person, ostensibly in the child's voice but in patently adult language, such as, "I can transition successfully throughout the day" or "I model subtraction by removing sets of 10 or fewer objects."

Checklist report cards such as these fail to communicate honest, thoughtful, and helpful assessments of children's learning. More fundamentally, the language used and the narrowness of their concepts of children's growth reflect destructive changes in curriculum and classroom expectations for young children. The reports are a window through which we can see a comparatively new view of kindergarten teaching, fueled by pressure from testing and mandates, most directly contradicting decades of observation and learning about young children's development.

Friedrich Froebel, the founder of the kindergarten in the 1830s, postulated that children grow and learn naturally by exploring materials creatively; participating socially with others; engaging in games, songs, and construction; learning by doing rather than following instructions (Froebel, 1826/1899). Froebel's ideas have since been confirmed and elaborated by generations of early childhood teachers and researchers. In violation of all this accumulated knowledge about early childhood development, creative arts and children's free exploration of materials are being sacrificed in the push for early academic achievement aimed at keeping children from "falling behind."

Although the clock can't be turned back and there is no prospect of a quick turnaround (though the history of American education suggests that eventually the pendulum may well swing back), teachers and parents who are appalled by the changed view of kindergarten need not feel completely hopeless. After examining some of what is happening to kindergartens, I discuss possibilities for small shifts within the classroom and cite cases of communities and educators who have joined together to push back against the current trends, sometimes succeeding in making positive changes in their schools. I base much of this discussion on my own experiences as a teacher but also on media reports, research, and conversation with other educators.

REPORTING TO PARENTS

While reports to parents may appear to be just a small part of teaching, the way we assess children and report to parents is inextricably linked to how we think about the children, their learning, and our teaching. The items chosen on the reports, the terms in which they are expressed, and the wording and intent of the grading scale used to categorize learning all present a particular view of how children learn. The reports are mirrors of standardized curricula and they convey to parents and teachers what schools expect. In a prescient article about report cards, Allan Shedlin, an educational reformer, wrote:

> If we agree that schools are learning communities where the pursuit of knowledge should be a vital and exciting activity, we would conclude that the schools seek to develop such qualities as creativity, inquisitiveness, perseverance, imagination, enthusiasm, flexibility, the ability to reason analytically, the ability to think abstractly, a willingness to make mistakes, the application of concepts and skills, the ability to perceive relationships and interrelationships, and the ability to function as a member of the community. . . . None of these qualities are presently included in most report cards. . . . The building of trust between home and school would surely be enhanced if, after reading a report card, a parent could exclaim, "They really know my child!" (Shedlin, 1988, p. 34)

At roughly the same time that Shedlin was writing this, I had very similar concerns. Writing about my own experiences as a practicing kindergarten teacher, I complained:

> Kindergarten used to mean brightly colored paintings, music, clay, block building, bursting curiosity, and intensive exploration. Now the kindergarten's exuberance is being muted, its color drained and spirit flattened, leaving us with stacks of paperwork and teacher manuals. No longer even designated "preschool," kindergarten is becoming an adjunct to 1st grade, with workbooks replacing art materials and formal instruction replacing activities that follow the children's interests. (Martin, 1985, p. 318)

After describing the varied ways that the children in my classroom were learning, I expressed my dread of a future in which "the art of teaching may be further eroded, and our children's potential for serious pursuit of knowledge may trickle away while the public rejoices in each decimal-point rise in standardized test scores" (Martin, 1985, p. 320).

SPECIOUS CHECKLISTS

Since currently much of the contact between parents and teachers in a conference centers on reports, we need to think carefully about how we report to parents. Checklists are deceptive in that they seem to cover all the ground there could possibly be—ground that often expands into yet further itemization with each new version of a checklist—while in reality they cut up a child's learning into such tiny bits of "skills" that you are left with multiple fragments and no picture of the whole child. Even with a few interspersed teacher comments, a checklist simply can't give you the flavor of a child's personality or experience in the classroom, much less an understanding of what and how that child is learning.

As I think of the children I taught over the years, I can see discrepancies between my observations about their learning and the way they would be evaluated in terms of checklist scoring. Bobby's persistent efforts to draw dinosaurs accurately, copying from books arranged around him on the table, were his way of learning about animals, nature, a historic time. But Bobby's use of art to gain knowledge couldn't be checked off under "creates art from imagination and memory," the closest item in one kindergarten checklist under "Fundamental Art Skill Development." Neither could Sandy's astounding inventiveness with arts and crafts materials and her expert skill at handling tools like scissors or needle and thread, which resulted in some spectacular collages, be summed up in an item like "uses art tools, materials and processes appropriately and successfully," which doesn't convey anything about this particular child's art work beyond the implication that she doesn't throw clay or spill paint.

Carol, who had constant disagreements with other children, would not have scored high in "shows awareness and responds appropriately to the feelings of others," but through daily concentrated play with toy animals alongside other children, she taught herself to negotiate social contacts, to find appropriate dialogue, and to sustain relationships. It is important to recognize Carol's specific efforts to learn "social skills" in her own way, through dramatic play with other children. But if dramatic play shows up at all in a typical checklist, it might be in a generalized statement like "engages in cooperative pretend play with another child." What we need to know is the particulars: What kind of pretend play? What characters does the child take on? What plot and dialogue emerge? What language is employed? How is the cooperation (or lack of it) demonstrated? Does the child like to perform for others? And if the child never engages in pretend play, what other means are used to express her ideas? Is she a builder? A painter? A dancer? A poet?

Items that end up in checklist reports may sound professional and all-inclusive but turn out to be irrelevant or uninformative when applied to particular students. "Generally and verbally expresses several possible solutions to a problem" cannot be separated from the kind of problem to be solved. Is it an interpersonal one? A mathematical one? A challenging assignment? Nancy was great at solving mathematical problems, but she had no idea about solving a personal conflict, or even realizing when she was provoking other children. Donald could get along with anyone and help others to work together, but dissolved into tears when faced with a hard puzzle. It is much more illuminating to note these details about children, and to describe the circumstances under which they cope easily or have a hard time, than to make undifferentiated generalizations.

Not only do the checklists fail to add insight and tend to give an inaccurate picture of a child, but many of the items are not really answerable by a check mark. Some are so general that they are meaningless: "takes appropriate risks" (What risks? In what areas?), "chooses to write" (What is the content and purpose of the chosen writing?), or "makes comparisons and points out relationships" (Comparisons of what? Under which circumstances?). Other items are so narrow that they are susceptible to daily changes, such as "repeats rhymes," "can lace, tie, button, zip," or "stands in line without bumping."

Some items are so grandiose that it's hard to know what they mean. A 1st-grade report contained only three science items (plus one for effort), the third one reading: "understands life, earth/space or physical science." Pretty tall order for a 6-year-old. In a kindergarten report, one heading is "Data Analysis, Statistics and Probability" under which the single item reads: "collects, sorts, organizes and draws conclusions about data." Some items seem to reduce a whole area of subject matter into triviality; for example, a 1st-grade report had only one item under the heading Geography: "explains that places can be found on maps and globes." Others appear to misunderstand the purposes of a field of study, such as this single item under the heading Economics: "begins to understand that hard work is needed to accomplish a task."

Then there are some items that are quite puzzling. In a draft form of one kindergarten checklist, this item (fortunately omitted in a later draft) was entered under Reading Enjoyment and Involvement: "appears to read or actually reads a book." Doesn't it matter which? Shouldn't a teacher know the difference? One checklist passed on to me about a child from another school system had items like "Quarrelsome," "Disobedient," "Chronically tense," "Destructive," and "Apathetic" to be graded on a scale of Outstanding, Average, or Weak—a step into the realm of pure absurdity.

Significantly, many of the new standards-based reports ignore the arts altogether or include some small token sections near the end, obviously considering the arts to be less important than the long lists of items about math and language. One kindergarten report contained 87 items, of which the last two read "participates in the visual arts" and "participates in movement and singing activities." Yet early childhood research and study generally support the important finding that young children learn by expressing themselves through the arts—painting, drawing, sculpture, crafts, dance, movement, drama, building, music, singing, rhythms, storytelling, poetry. The arts are not extra frills to stick onto the end of a reporting form, almost as an afterthought. They provide the basic experiences that inform learning in all areas of study. For two trenchant descriptions of how children learn through the arts and how teachers can use this knowledge in the classroom, see *Considering Children's Art: Why and How to Value Their Works* (Engel, 1995) and *The Languages of Learning* (Gallas, 1994).

There is no way to separate learning in mathematics, language, literature, science, or anything else from the arts. Children's growing capacities to observe, represent, understand, and describe are at the heart of learning and teaching in kindergarten (and should continue to be further along in school as well). Through building tall structures with the blocks every day, Jon is learning about relationships of shapes, balance, weight, and symmetry. Though he may be thinking more about the aesthetics and play value of the building, this is certainly basic math and science learning. It is probably more important at this stage of mathematical awareness than being able to "count orally backward 20–0." But block building or other construction is not considered important enough to even mention.

There is a disturbing disconnect between a learning community within a classroom highly responsive to individual learners and the narrow numerical assessments. A teacher may be committed to supporting individual learning styles and offering a rich array of materials and projects that draw in children whose levels and interests range widely. However, the written report presented to the parents, and filed for posterity, may reflect very little of each child's actual experience in the class. Agonizing over how to fill in checklists, teachers may feel frustrated that so little of what they know about the children comes through and that each child's particular strengths, accomplishments, talents, and vulnerabilities are not only almost impossible to garner from the multitude of small items rated but are often left out of the picture entirely.

FLAWED EXPECTATIONS

In the preparation of curriculum, testing, and reporting, there is generally the assumption that children's learning proceeds in orderly steps, progressing in a particular sequence of understanding and mastery of material. The items teachers are asked to check on their reports measure children in terms of where they are supposed to be at a certain age and time in their lives. However, while there are evidently developmental levels and milestones in children's learning, there are enough variations among individual children's progress to make the application of a predetermined sequence of levels misleading. Children are forever surprising us with sudden jumps back and forth in their knowledge and understanding. They learn in the context of what interests and holds them, and they may acquire skills as they need them, in a different order from the assumed sequence.

Ordinary life in the classroom can produce unexpected happenings that make us more aware of children's abilities, temperaments, and uneven learning. One day Lewis, one of the youngest boys in my kindergarten class—as yet unskilled in reading or writing—went to the computer with a friend and together they managed to produce a picture and a one-sentence story recorded by Lewis's friend: "Me and Lewis went to the park." Lewis was very proud of this effort and then asked to act it out as we often did with stories the children wrote. I was a bit surprised but said he could. After the "story" was read aloud to the class, Lewis stood up authoritatively and said, "Who will be the sun?" (There was a sun in the picture.) "Who will be the flowers? Who will be the snails?" As children eagerly volunteered, we got more animals (such as horses!) and pretty soon everybody had a part, including one child who was asked to be the slide. Lewis and his friend walked around among the other children, and the different groups of animals started to make up songs—a flower song from a pair of children, a hissing snake song from another child. It was a lovely spontaneous performance that went on for about 10 minutes, and one I never would have thought of from the sentence that Lewis and his friend had written. Evidently, behind the sparse text there was a whole teeming world in Lewis's mind, and he was able to communicate it to the other children and inspire them to create a musical tableau on the spot.

There are no little boxes on checklists that correspond to this demonstration of Lewis's imaginative use of story and drama, nor of his desire to enact his personal vision with the whole class and his organizational skill as a producer and director. The items taken from actual kindergarten reports such as "uses clear oral language and complete sentences when speaking" or even "composes story using own ideas" wouldn't accurately reflect what Lewis was doing—nor would "participates in group oral composition" or "attempts to tell a story." Moreover, on a checklist report card, what would probably stand out would be his deficiencies in reading and writing skills.

DESTRUCTION OF KINDERGARTEN

These checklists are not only inadequate reporting formats, but reflect a changed curriculum for kindergarten children, through which a focus on discrete academic skills has supplanted the traditional emphasis on social, intellectual, and personal growth. The significance of the newest trends in kindergarten checklist reporting lies in the pernicious changes in kindergarten programs themselves, the disregard of young children's needs and development, and the advent of unrealistic expectations for our youngest students expressed in terms of test scores and school entrance requirements.

In some schools the introduction of standardized tests to children as young as preschool age has exerted such pressures that the school justifies wholly inappropriate lessons in the name of preparing for the tests. In 2003, the federal government instituted national standardized testing in verbal and math skills for all Head Start programs. By December 2007, after years of controversy about the inappropriate testing of 3- and 4-year-olds, the Head Start reauthorization bill eliminated the requirement of testing Head Start children.

Kindergartens, however, are still targeted for testing, and curriculum is geared to that. In school systems all over the country, kindergartens are using elaborate phonics reading programs and introducing curriculum that used to be considered 1st- and 2nd-grade material. In response, some worried parents are delaying kindergarten entrance for their perfectly competent children—"redshirting" them—for fear they won't be able to perform well enough to compete with their classmates (Paul, 2010).

The long-standing controversies about cutoff dates for kindergarten entrance generally resulted in raising the entrance age in many communities and giving screening tests to entering students. Where the younger children were not screened out into readiness classes or held back a year, they were expected to perform at the same level as the older, more mature ones with often a year or more difference in age within a class, which is, after all, a fifth of the life of a 5-year-old. When one kindergarten teacher tried to explain that children learn to read at different times and in different ways according to each child's development, she was told by a reading program supervisor, "We don't do developmental anymore."

Fortunately, in spite of the push for early academic achievement, there are still strong voices speaking up in defense of childhood play as an essential element of school success and decrying the change in kindergarten programs. In an extensive, well-researched kindergarten report, the Alliance for Childhood states:

> Kindergarten has changed radically in the last two decades in ways that few Americans are aware of. Children now spend far more time being taught and tested on literacy and math skills than they do learning through play and exploration, exercising their bodies, and using their imaginations. Many kindergartens use highly prescriptive curricula geared to new state standards and linked to standardized tests. In an increasing number of kindergartens, teachers must follow scripts from which they may not deviate. These practices, which are not well grounded in research, violate long-established principles of child development and good teaching. It is clear that they are compromising both children's health and their long-term prospects for success in school (Miller & Almon, 2009, p. 11).

In what sounds like an echo of my lament a quarter century earlier, the introduction ends, "Kindergarten has ceased to be a garden of delight and has become a place of stress and distress."

WHAT IS TO BE DONE?

The transformation of kindergarten away from individualized learning and toward standardized instruction raises an urgent question for teachers who, from their own experience and training, understand what is being sacrificed: How can we continue to work in public education and not give in to despair? And further, what can we do to make changes, keep ourselves from being drawn into enacting what we don't believe, and yet retain our teaching jobs? How do we hold on to our visions of maintaining a rich educational setting and attention to individual needs in spite of restrictive and mistaken notions of how young children learn? Are there areas where teachers can raise their voices, be heard, and make a difference?

Perhaps the best way to start is to look at children and remind ourselves of why we went into teaching in the first place and how gratifying (if exhausting) it is to live with young children in the classroom. Although schools have changed, little children have not. They are still the same lively, unpredictable, enthusiastic learners who manage to find ways to express themselves and play out their imaginings, if only by inventing secret dialogues between their pencils and erasers. To give scope to children's imagination, even in minor ways, to keep alive the spark of learning and creativity is probably a teacher's first mandate, outweighing the mandates for teachers that come down from the top.

Giving children the opportunity to learn from each other and to use materials creatively requires thoughtful provisioning of materials; a room arrangement that is organized so that children can find what they need and keep things in place; and, most of all, time for children to learn to make choices and for the teacher to attend to what the children are doing. The opportunity to choose from a variety of materials and activities opens the way for children to immerse themselves in learning by their own motivation, their own ways and rhythms. When children experiment with materials, work on projects of their own devising, pursue their interests and study subjects in depth, they become far more involved in their education than when they are only carrying out tasks presented by teachers. With all the curriculum demands placed on kindergarten classes, it may seem almost impossible to make space for self-directed learning and to squeeze in any activities beyond those mandated. But even the busiest schedule or most rigid curriculum must leave at least short bursts of time that can be seized to give the children some weekly or (preferably) daily periods where they can make free choices among materials in the room. Where no art or "play" materials are available, there are sources for scrounging: natural objects found outdoors even in cities (seeds, leaves, caterpillars); household discards to recycle, like cardboard tubes, bits of gift wrap, wood scraps (parents usually respond well to scrounge lists from teachers); wallpaper books; industrial waste items that turn up in recycling centers or children's museums. Add some bottles of glue and, if possible, some paints and tape, and children will create their own "inventions" and collages, engage in dramatic play, study seeds and growing plants, observe caterpillars turning into butterflies. Plastic basins can be filled with salt, sand, or water; and empty yogurt cups, shampoo bottles, and other containers can be used for filling and pouring. Eyedroppers and food-colored water make for hours of color mixing (or concocting "potions"). An appeal to the school community can yield donations of outgrown toys, books, and building sets. There are endless ways for enterprising teachers to collect interesting, stimulating materials without spending much of their hard-won earnings.

Provided that there are even small amounts of free time to be snatched, and that the room is provisioned even minimally, children can be helped to learn to make choices among materials and activities to produce art work, build, enact dramas, read books, write stories, sing and dance, play games, do puzzles, sew, talk with each other, make science observations, come up with new ideas and discoveries. In short, they will be learning from each other and from the interaction with materials.

Once some free-choice times have been established and children have learned to become more or less independent in their activities, the teacher is free to circulate around the room and do what is seldom done by administrators or producers of mandated curriculum—namely, to closely observe individuals and groups of children over time and record what is happening in the classroom. Teachers are full of stories about "their" children and the high drama that goes on in the kindergarten classroom every day. By writing down these observations, teachers can build up valuable knowledge that is helpful for better understanding individual children, planning classroom projects, reporting to parents, working with specialists, talking to administrators.

If this kind of free-choice period is frowned upon or even explicitly disapproved by school administrations, perhaps it can be done at a time when nobody is apt to come by the room. Even better, teachers can explain how such activities are part of a particular curriculum project or learning concept that is included within the guidelines. Articulate explanations combined with evidence of the children's learning (art, writing, teacher notes, photos, or video) furnish eloquent proof of the value of providing choice periods. Student teachers, classroom aides, and parents can be recruited to help with the documentation by taking photos of ephemeral accomplishments like amazing block buildings and designs or by recording or videotaping children's plays, discussions, music, or dance.

Skills of observation, description, and documentation can be learned by doing and are further honed when teachers come together to build their knowledge of children and of teaching practice. Typically, teachers have tended to be isolated in their classrooms with little chance for contact with colleagues. Where there have been efforts by teachers to seek out colleagues who are willing to meet regularly for discussion, the participants have often found strength and revitalization. They have also been able to clarify their ideas and register their dissatisfaction with mandated practices that they find harmful to children and their learning. Report cards and curricula are not writ in stone, and there may be more room for change and revision than teachers realize. When teachers join together, especially alongside parents, community members, and child development experts, their combined voices may make themselves heard. Speaking up at meetings and in committees, talking with parents and parent groups, writing letters to administrators and local papers can yield results. Writing is a particularly powerful weapon, even on an individual basis, and can sometimes push the recipients to further thought or even reconsideration.

For instance, in one Massachusetts city the school administration instituted a pilot program to test a new standards-based progress report. The parents, many of whom had evidently been blindsided, responded with protests. They attended school committee meetings, wrote letters to the administration, and expressed their disapproval in an email survey. There were also objections from teachers: "We were repeatedly told that our comments were subjective and not needed." Members of the Progress Report Committee spoke out as well, stating, "We see joyful, exciting learning going on in every classroom. This report drains all that away" (Crudele, 1995). The strong critical reaction was enough to get the administration to abandon their new progress report even before the end of the year and return to an earlier form that was not as lengthy and had much more space for teacher comments. While the earlier form was not ideal either, the combined efforts of parents and teachers managed to hold back the worst of the standards-based report wave in their schools.

Teachers joining together can sometimes achieve changes. In San Diego, kindergarten teachers formed a Kindergarten Leadership Team and fought for 2 years against what they felt were inappropriate and harmful benchmarks for literacy and math. Although their opinion was not shared by all the parents and teachers, they made a strong push at a school-board meeting to make the benchmarks more age-appropriate, and "the board voted 3–2 for the change after a faction of teachers said the district's academically intensive curriculum for 4- and 5-year-olds is unrealistic and oppressive" (Gao, 2005).

In Seattle, teachers, students, and parents joined together to protest against a standardized test in reading and math that they found wasteful and harmful to students. Starting with a boycott of the test in one high school, the movement spread to other schools and got nationwide attention, with support from prominent educators. After many months, the school board backed down, saying the MAP test would now be optional for high schools, as long as the schools found other ways to evaluate students.

In many other parts of the country there have also been strong parent and teacher protests against high-stakes testing; cutting of funds to education; wholesale closings of schools, particularly in poor communities; and removing arts and physical education programs from the curriculum. There is a growing national movement of resistance by parents and teachers to what is happening to children in restrictive settings and to the impact of standardization and the relentless push for "data collection" and score-based assessment on public schools.

While there is much to discourage teachers in the current educational climate, there are evidently possibilities for change on many levels—making small changes in the classroom, writing and speaking up wherever possible, joining with others to achieve specific changes, supporting schools and school systems that are working to develop alternatives to standards-based programs. If the combined knowledge of people working with young children can add up to a public indictment of current mandates and to a revival of early childhood teaching values that have been summarily discarded, perhaps it could lead to a national movement to bring kindergarten back to its original mission of developing every child's capacity as a learner and social being. Then we could stop reducing kindergartens to factories for fragmented skill production and reinstate early childhood classes that are vibrant gardens where all children can grow and flourish. And, who knows, perhaps after that we may even be able to extend the democratic ideal of developing every child's capacity from kindergarten to encompass all levels in America's schools.

Conclusion

Ellen Schwartz

What does it mean that teachers in a beleaguered school in North Philadelphia, a school that was put into "turnaround" and ultimately closed, held onto their books, hiding them in a custodian's closet? The school itself, from its very opening, challenged the status quo, as Betsy Wice recounts in this book. The school had a legacy, with roots in Black history. It is as telling as it is ironic that teachers at Douglass would turn to subterfuge to keep literacy alive. I highlight this example because it puts into stark relief the realities of public education in the 21st century, especially in poor communities and communities of color. The school was closed. But it's no small matter that colleagues from Douglass "continue to share books with each other and with the children."

The press to "raise achievement" is creating a sense of panic in the United States about our educational system. This is palpable in Peg Howes's Review of Practice. It is what threatens to throw her off course, to pull her away from what she can reliably count on in teaching: knowledge of the children. This translates to pressure on children, on teachers, and on families. It also translates to desperate searches for the perfect fix, the set of standards or instructional program that will get all those children "up over the bar." My own school, like many, is cluttered with disused programs that were touted, not so many years ago, as *the thing* that would solve our math problem, our reading problem, our spelling problem. Eventually they find their way into the Dumpster. Unlike Douglass School's books, they are not worth saving.

In the face of these realities, of what use are these stories, this view of educating that is at odds with current policy? In particular, of what use are they to teachers struggling to make their way in the ever-changing ground of public education?

A HUNGER AMONG TEACHERS

When Prospect Center closed, its Archives were donated to Special Collections at the University of Vermont. With a gift from Prospect, the University established fellowships for practitioners and researchers to work with the Archives. In the first 2 years, 10 teachers from early childhood centers, public schools, and independent schools have been granted practitioner fellowships. I've had the privilege of working with these teachers—some quite new to teaching—as they explored the records of the School and Center.

What I have discovered through working with the Fellows is that there is a hunger among teachers for something that acknowledges both the intellectual and relational work of teaching. In the first summer of the UVM Fellowships, I had assumed from people's applications that they would be interested in documentation of things like curriculum, formation of group, and teacher interviews. They were, but what took me by surprise was the passion aroused by the more philosophical writings, essays that described a way of thinking about children and learning that resonated with their own deeply held values.

Equally, the Fellows were drawn to the history of Prospect School— to imagine it as a school in action and also to understand its origins and changes. An early "scrapbook" designed to introduce the school to a larger community was tagged as a gem for its explanation of the move away from the English Infant School model. Some teachers noted that the narrative records weren't always descriptive, sometimes lapsing into judgmental language, and they wondered about that. Another found a very early version of the Staff Review that seemed so different from the Descriptive Review of the Child as we know it today. The questions raised by these materials served as a reminder that the archives reveal a school in process, with all the contradictions and imperfections that implies.

Prospect opened in 1965, a time when public education was being infused with new ideas and energy. U.S. educators were learning from the British Infant Schools, and projects such as the Elementary Science Study were springing up domestically, challenging teachers to rethink learning and teaching. In Prospect's home state, the Vermont Design for Education was developed by the State Department of Education. This farsighted document set forth goals for public education that were consonant with Prospect's philosophy of recognition of the student as a person, of trust in the desire of all humans to learn, and of an education built on children's strengths, questions, and interests (Vermont State Department of Education, 1971). This was unfolding at a time when other challenges to the status quo were being raised by the civil rights movement, the anti–Vietnam War movement, and the women's movement, to name a few.

Then, as now, there was resistance. Then, as now, the backlash centered on "accountability." Then, as now, testing was offered as the solution to so-called failing schools. Vito Perrone, convener of the North Dakota Study Group on Evaluation, recalled that era: "By 1977, competency tests were in place in thirty-six states, with the need to meet some related score for promotion and graduation firmly in place" (Engel, 2005, p. 32). The move to greater standardization ramped up in the 1980s in response to *A Nation at Risk* (U.S. National Commission on Excellence in Education, 1983).

During these years, Prospect's narrative and descriptive approaches to record-keeping offered an alternative to teachers searching for ways to document what was going on in their classrooms, which is detailed in Lynne Strieb's chapter in this book. Prospect's disciplined modes of keeping track of children, their work, and their learning explicitly valued the teacher's intimate knowledge of children and the classroom. It was this documentation—alongside the philosophical writings—that excited such interest among the UVM Fellows, suggesting new avenues of inquiry in their own practice. Looking at documentation of children and of curriculum, a teacher from a New York City public school saw ways to make fuller use of her own school's collections of children's work to inform her choices about materials and curriculum. Another teacher, this one from an early childhood center, was captivated by documentation of a children's discussion about change—living, growing, and dying—and shared this with colleagues at her center, sparking interest in doing descriptive work with the young children they teach.

THINKING SPACE

The stories, essays, and interviews in this book are intended to "make space" for readers to consider their own practice, the choices they make, and the options open to them and the young people they teach. Sometimes teachers are prompted to examine their practice because something isn't working out for a child or because a teacher is experiencing conflicts of value. This was the case with Peg Howes, whose Review of Practice began with the wake-up call about assessment that Sam presented. For Regina Ritscher, it was Aidan's ability to do mental math that he couldn't explain, which, as she put it, "stopped me in my tracks," leading to a study of both Aidan *and* math assessment. Bruce Turnquist's discomfort with placing his students on grids, and his worry that Alice would fail to be seen in her complexity in that "efficient" system, sparked his Review of Practice.

But there is something more. The questions raised in this book about children, classrooms, and schools point to larger educational and human issues. What do rubrics say about the meaning of work and its relation to the maker, and what are the implications for assessment? What does the "gridding" of children mean in terms of how we value them and the immense range present in any group? What values about learning and humanness are communicated through checklists? What is lost when play is curtailed or when a child's home language is not welcome in school?

These are philosophical questions, questions about the meaning inherent in decisions and actions. From its inception, Prospect emphasized the importance of philosophy for schools. In her essay "Making and Doing Philosophy in a School," Patricia Carini recounts what it meant to enact philosophy in the midst of the everyday life of a school. She asserts that "the source from which philosophies spring is a *burning human desire* . . . to make sense of the world" (Carini & Himley, 2010, p. 155). At Prospect School, what this meant is that observations didn't just sit on a shelf gathering dust. Rather, they were studied with an eye to meaning. In one story retold in the essay, staff at the school came together to better understand what was going on with a child who, unpredictably, seemed to fly into rages. Looking more closely, they began to question what it meant to label his actions as "rage." In shifting their focus and continuing to observe the child, they came to understand that he was a child capable of great persistence and intensity and that what he was expressing was "not so much rage as need for an emotional release—an outlet for overwrought feeling" (Carini & Himley, 2010, p. 161). This, in turn, led to changes in their appreciation of him and their work with him.

As Peg Howes says in the Afterthoughts to her Review of Practice, there are superficial similarities between the Review process and the problem-solving protocols commonplace in many schools. In both cases there is a desire to take action, to make things better. The starting points, however, are vastly different. What Prospect offers teachers is a space to lay out their thinking in the company of others, looking closely at particular evidence (data, if you will) such as children's work, classroom materials, and teaching records and notes. The aim is not so much to solve a problem as to help the teacher to rethink an aspect of practice. At the same time, this deepening of understanding is intimately connected to action. As Jessica Howard, a long-time Prospect teacher, puts it, the work of descriptive inquiry "clears the deck for action." There is also an acknowledgment that there really is no ending point, no point at which the teacher can say that the "problem" is solved, no point at which the teacher might not be surprised (or even blindsided) by an unexpected turn of events.

The classrooms portrayed in this book are places where children are taken seriously as strivers after meaning, and the children's own wonderings and ideas are folded into curriculum. The teachers are also searching for meaning. Teaching 1st graders about silkworms, learning alongside them, observing and documenting their talk, leads Rhoda Kanevsky to raise questions about what can be learned through observation and description—not just for her students, but also in the discipline of science—which in turn leads her to the work of Barbara McClintock. For Kiran Chaudhuri, an inquiry that begins with one adolescent with a tenuous connection to school expectations branches out into an expansive inquiry into the meaning of valued work and the relationship of "evidence" to work. The exploration of questions such as these, with ongoing interweaving of inquiry and practice, is what creates the possibility for teaching to be ever generative, renewing, and invigorating.

The view of teaching set forth in this book is intimate and individual, rooted always in relationship. There is, first and foremost, the teacher's relationship with the young people in his or her care. To value a teacher's knowledge of his or her students is to recognize that understanding of others is born of close relationship and to claim space for teaching as a human activity. It is to acknowledge that teachers can discern their students' values and standards, and their own, and that these have more to do with what Kiran Chaudhuri calls "valued work" than standards handed down from afar. It is to privilege descriptions that bring a child to life over scores that render the child—and the teacher—invisible.

The Descriptive Review of Practice, like all of Prospect's descriptive processes, is collaborative in nature, recognizing that it is through connections with others that a teacher stands to gain a fresh take on his or her own practice. Even when a full-scale Review is not possible, talking with a few colleagues can add perspective. When a support teacher asked Ann Caren, "How can Justin work on his own with so many people checking in to help him?" it was through talking together that the adults working with Justin came up with a plan to foster his independence.

To value teaching as human and relational work means recognizing that it can be as "messy" as we humans sometimes are. It means, too, that teachers and children alike will experience conflicts of value, that the way ahead won't necessarily be a straight, clear path. In this era when efficiency and standardization guide much of what is touted as "education reform," how do we make space for a messier, more complicated understanding of teaching and learning—particularly in the education of new teachers?

IN THE COMPANY OF OTHERS

One of the educators working with new teachers to help them gain a nuanced understanding of teaching is Mary Hebron, associate director of the Art of Teaching Program at Sarah Lawrence College (SLC). In her 2011 Wright Lecture at SLC, she told a story that provides a glimpse into another era, not so long ago:

> In 1974 . . . I was hired to teach kindergarten in Greenburgh, New York. There I
> was mentored by a staff of amazing veteran teachers and a thoughtful and gifted
> principal, Rena Hirsch, who spoke with me every morning, often for more than
> an hour before my kindergarteners arrived, about the particular children in my

class and about how to engage them as thinkers and learners. Our morning conversations enabled me to say aloud what I was hoping to accomplish in my teaching. Her wise, nonjudgmental guidance influenced me then and is still present in my work today. . . . Each day my more experienced colleagues came to my classroom to ask how things were going, to talk about a child, to offer an idea or borrow one. . . . My principal and the teachers in Greenburgh provided me with an understanding of what it means to belong to a teaching community that has trust in the capacity of all children, and even in that of a novice teacher. I learned that teaching is complex, layered work that is not easily done without the company and collaboration of others who are also deeply engaged in work with children. (Hebron, 2011)

From today's vantage point, this story is striking for the way in which a new teacher was brought along by her more experienced colleagues. Rather than receiving training in the implementation of a teaching program "adopted" by her school, Mary was invited into conversation with both her principal and colleagues, conversation rooted in actual classroom experiences. She was brought into the intellectual and relational work of teaching by having the opportunity to think aloud about children with her principal and colleagues. What she remembers after all these years are these conversations, and the "nonjudgmental guidance" she received. Her story echoes that of Sister Seema, told in the Introduction to this book.

Mary carries these early teaching experiences into her work in Sarah Lawrence's Art of Teaching Program. Knowing the children is the starting point of the program, which is rooted in Prospect's philosophy and descriptive processes. As Mary explains, "We begin in the Observation and Documentation course by emphasizing the importance of local knowledge, that is, knowledge made about particular children and their particular strengths and capacities, gained through careful, respectful observation" (Hebron, 2011). This leads, inevitably, to rethinking curriculum and to questions about what it means to draw on this knowledge of children while negotiating the school, district, and state expectations.

Mary and her colleagues know that graduates of her program will make compromises, as they themselves do in order to prepare teachers for the realities of 21st-century public schools. Their aim is to prepare teachers who will be clear-eyed about the choices they have and the compromises they make. Through intensive work in observation, description, reflection, and documentation they strive to give them "a foundation that . . . will enable them to 'hold their centers' and keep an eye open for those places where space can be made for the children and their work" (Hebron, 2011).

The Art of Teaching program is preparing the next generation of teachers in much the same spirit that inspired the contributors to this book. The ability to see those cracks, those spaces where action can be taken, is explicit in Prospect's philosophy. As Patricia Carini expresses it, "It is by sustaining a philosophical attitude, by reflecting, recollecting, questioning, that it is possible to face threatened loss and to reach decisions on when to resist, on how not to give one more inch than necessary, and on how to make what inches you have count for a lot" (Carini & Himley, 2010, p. 165).

THE VALUE OF STRUGGLE

With teachers under attack, near-daily announcements of public school closures, and school districts scrambling for the funding to keep schools staffed, it is easy to become demoralized or cynical. Finding "wiggle room" and making "small changes" may seem like a drop in the bucket. Perhaps not worth the effort when we are so far from ensuring that all children have access to a spacious education—not to speak of food, healthcare, housing, and other fundamental rights. When we are so far from achieving these aims, how can the "small" classroom changes make a difference?

The very act of working toward more just and humane education is itself of value. There are times when that struggle takes place on a broad scale, in the public arena: the 2011 occupation of the Wisconsin State House, the refusal of Garfield High School teachers in Seattle to give the Measures of Academic Progress tests, the resistance of teachers and community members in Chicago to public school closures and budget cuts. There are, likewise, times when struggle is enacted in the classroom or school: "small" actions that make it possible for a child's strengths to be recognized, for a group of children to explore their own questions, for a group of adolescents to discover their own capacities to "do history." These are not insignificant.

As Patricia Carini puts it:

Prospect's philosophy holds that struggle itself has positive value, is indeed itself a worthy work, and more than that, a work indispensable to the well-being of society. As a work in its own right, struggle, like teaching, can anticipate no final destination, no final solution. There is always more to be done, for there is no conceivable conclusion to the striving for a more just society, more equal distribution of opportunity, for schools that are more (not less) roomy. For those dedicated to the proposition that the world or the society at large can be more humane, there isn't going to be a time to say with satisfaction, "Well, we solved that problem," and dusting off our hands, depart from the scene. There isn't going to be a time when advocacy and struggle can be set aside. (personal communication, June 26, 2012)

This book offers a vision of what is possible when teachers sustain the struggle for education that builds on the strengths of children and teachers. It is a vision that recognizes the power of doing this work in relationship with others, both young people and colleagues. It is a vision that honors the desire we all have to do work of value and meaning, work that holds open space to be awakened to unanticipated possibility.

This book also invites action, both in the classroom and in the larger arena of educational policy and politics. It is a call to keep alive an education that is rooted in children's interests. It is a call to trust in each child's capacity for "big learning" and to make space for each child to contribute. It is a call to join with others in resisting incursions on the human relationships and human understandings that constitute the art of teaching.

Appendix: Prospect's Descriptive Review of Practice

This version of the Review of Practice format is adapted by Rhoda Kanevsky and Lynne Strieb from earlier versions developed at Prospect School and Center.

PURPOSE

The primary purpose of the Descriptive Review of Practice is to offer the teacher an opportunity to describe and reflect on his or her current work within the context of the teacher's personal history, the teacher's early visions and goals for him- or herself, and the possible constraints the teacher faces in fulfilling these goals in his or her current setting. A teacher may have a particular concern about his or her practice and may use this process to address that concern. Because the Descriptive Review of Practice occurs in a collaborative setting that offers multiple perspectives on the teacher's work, he or she may uncover new ways of fulfilling the visions of teaching that inspired him or her to be a teacher in the first place.

For the participants, a Descriptive Review of Practice will add to their understanding of the nature of teaching, what is fulfilling to a teacher, and what is central and indispensable to the work of teaching.

PREPARING FOR THE REVIEW

The shape and procedure for the Descriptive Review of Practice is designed anew for each occasion through a conversation between the teacher and the person who will chair the review. Since the formulation of the framing question is key to other procedural decisions, time taken to arrive at a satisfactory formulation of that issue is time well spent. One to two conversations between the teacher and the chairperson will be needed to arrive at a well-organized plan for the review.

The review is intended to be limited to approximately 2 hours. Usually the teacher's presentation takes about an hour; another hour is needed for questions, discussion, comments, and suggestions.

THE REVIEW SESSION

Chair's Introduction

The chair convenes the session by having participants introduce themselves and emphasizing confidentiality, then sets the stage by describing the components of the Review and any background necessary to understand the teacher's setting. This generally includes brief demographic information about the school, the age of children and/or subject(s) taught by the presenting teacher, and any other relevant contextual information, along with an outline of the teacher's current duties and work history.

The chair then states the focusing question for the Review and suggests that participants jot down questions and thoughts as they listen to the presenting teacher, whose description of practice will be uninterrupted.

Teacher's Description of Practice

The teacher's presentation usually starts with background information more specific than what the chair has provided. This often includes a floor plan of the classroom and typical daily schedule. It may also include the teacher's reflection on how teaching was chosen as a work; important influences (positive and negative) on the teacher's philosophy, practice, and personal growth; interests apart from teaching; other vocations attractive to the teacher now or in the past; values or ideas important to the teacher and, possibly, their sources in childhood or adolescence.

The teacher's description may be based on some of the elements below, or others relevant to his or her situation, and is organized under the headings developed in the planning process.

- the teacher's hopes and expectations for the children
- the shape and rhythm of the work of teaching on a daily, weekly, quarterly basis
- materials and classroom activities at the center of the teacher's practice, the teacher's understanding of how a curriculum evolves
- how the teacher gets to know the children; how the teacher sees him- or herself in relation to the children; how the teacher envisions the children's relationships to each other

- how the teacher reflects on teaching; who and what offers support for reflection
- those aspects of practice that are most satisfying, most challenging, most frustrating
- those aspects of practice that are most reliable, least developed, on the periphery of the teacher's thinking
- the teacher's aspirations and the teacher's sense of the gap between those aspirations and actual practice; the factors that prevent closing that gap and the supports that facilitate achieving those aims
- the values the teacher understands to be at the root of his or her practice and the teacher's own standards for teaching

Woven into the teacher's description may be materials or artifacts associated with his or her teaching life that the teacher has brought to the session.

Colleagues' Observations

If colleagues are present, they may be invited to briefly add observations or commentary about their sense of the presenting teacher's stance, relationships, interests, and standards.

Integrative Restatement

The chair gathers the main threads of the teacher's presentation.

Clarifying Questions

The chair invites participants to ask questions of the presenter. These are intended to draw out fuller description and to clarify any points of confusion for participants.

Integrative Restatement

The chair summarizes the main themes from this discussion.

Responses to Focusing Question

The chair restates the focusing question, after which participants make responses to it. These may take the form of suggestions, but equally they may be participants' reflections on the terrain opened up by the question and its meaning for the teacher.

Process Discussion

After the Review itself, the chair invites comments to process. The presenting teacher may comment on his or her experience of preparing and presenting the review. Other participants reflect on what the experience was like for them and ask any questions they may have about the process itself. The chair ends the session by restating the necessity of confidentiality.

THE ROLE OF THE CHAIR

The chairperson convenes the review, describes the plan, and assigns a note-taker to record the integrative restatements and participants' responses to the focusing question. The chair is responsible for announcing all major transitions within the presentation and inserting integrative restatements at the relevant points.

The chair has a major responsibility for safeguarding respect for the presenting teacher by ensuring that the group stays descriptive throughout. The presenting teacher is in a vulnerable position because the teacher is exposing him- or herself, through his or her teaching practice, to the group. If the chair feels that the group is veering away from description into speculation or outright judgment, it is the chair's responsibility to interrupt the session to call attention to this and to get the group back on track.

References

Aardema, V. (1977). *Who's in Rabbit's house?* New York, NY: Dial Books for Young Readers.

Alexander, R. B. (1998). *Changing bodies, changing lives: A book for teens on sex and relationships.* New York, NY: Times Books.

Andrias, J., Kanevsky, R. D., Strieb, L. Y., & Traugh, C. (1992). *Exploring values and standards: Implications for assessment.* New York, NY: National Center for Restructuring Education, Schools, and Teaching.

Atwell, N. (1998) *In the middle.* Portsmouth, NH: Boynton/Cook.

Banks, R. (1995). *Rule of the bone.* New York, NY: HarperCollins.

Beaver, J. (2006). *Developmental reading assessment.* Parsippany, NJ: Celebration Press.

Benjamin, A. (1992). *Young Harriet Tubman: Freedom fighter.* Mahwah, NJ: Troll Associates.

Buck, P. (1994) *The good earth.* New York, NY: Washington Square Press (Original work published 1931).

Burns, M. (1991). *Math by all means: Multiplication grade 3.* Sausalito, CA: Math Solutions Publications.

Byrne, J., Chichester, D. G., & Marz, R. (1996) *The Amalgam age of comics.* New York, NY: DC Comics.

Carini, P. F. (2001). *Starting strong: A different look at children, schools, and standards.* New York, NY: Teachers College Press.

Carini, P. F., & Himley, M. (2010) *Jenny's story: Taking the long view of the child.* New York, NY: Teachers College Press.

Cisneros, S. (1991). *The house on Mango Street.* New York, NY: Vintage Books.

Cole, J. (1983). *Bony-legs.* New York, NY: Four Winds Press.

Crudele, L. (1995, April 27). New progress reports flunked. *Newton TAB,* p. 17.

D'Aulaire, I., & D'Aulaire, E. P. (1962). *D'Aulaire's Book of Greek Myths.* Garden City, NY: Doubleday.

Dewey, J. (1963). *Experience and education.* New York, NY: Collier Books (Original work published 1938)

Díaz, J. (1996). *Drown.* New York, NY: Riverhead Books.

Douglass, F. (1960). *Narrative of the life of Frederick Douglass, an American slave.* Cambridge, MA: Belknap Press (Original work published 1845).

Edwards, P. D. (1997). *Barefoot: Escape on the Underground Railroad.* New York, NY: HarperCollins.

Elkin, B. (1958). *The big jump and other stories*. New York, NY: Random House.

Elkin, B. (1960). *The king's wish and other stories*. New York, NY: Random House.

Engel, B. S. (1995). *Considering children's art: Why and how to value their works*. Washington, DC: National Association for the Education of Young Children.

Engel, B. S. (with Martin, A. C.) (Eds.). (2005). *Holding values: What we mean by progressive education*. Portsmouth, NH: Heinemann.

Ensor, H. (1970). *Altair design*. New York, NY: Pantheon.

Evans, M. A., Wenzel, P., & Wells, H. G. (1991). *The war of the worlds*. New York, NY: Random House.

Fauset, A. H. (1927). *For freedom*. Philadelphia, PA: Franklin.

Fleming, R. L. (1994). *The big book of urban legends: Adapted from the works of Jan Harold Brunvand*. New York, NY: Paradox Press.

Froebel, F. (1899). *The education of man* (M. Hailmann, Trans.) New York, NY: Appleton. (Original work published 1826)

Gallas, K. (1994). *The languages of learning*. New York, NY: Teachers College Press.

Ganske, K. (2000). *Word journeys: Assessment-guided phonics, spelling, and vocabulary instruction*. New York, NY: Guilford Press.

Gao, H. (2005, February 9). School board votes 3–2 on reading level required. *San Diego Union Tribune*. Retrieved from http://legacy.utsandiego.com

Gawande, A. (2013, July 29). Slow ideas. *The New Yorker, 89*(22), 36–45.

Gordimer, N. (1995). *Writing and being*. Cambridge, MA: Harvard University Press.

Hebron, M. (2011, July). *Voices of children, voices of teachers: Reclaiming the classroom*. Thomas H. Wright Lecture, Sarah Lawrence College, Bronxville, NY.

Hesse, K. (1997). *Out of the dust*. New York, NY: Scholastic Press.

Himley, M. (Ed.). (2011). *Prospect's descriptive processes: The child, the art of teaching, and the classroom and school* (Rev. ed.). Retrieved from http://cdi.uvm.edu

Himley, M. (with Carini, P. F.) (Eds.). (2000). *From another angle: Children's strengths and school standards*. New York, NY: Teachers College Press.

Hopkinson, D. (1993). *Sweet Clara and the freedom quilt*. New York, NY: Knopf.

Jackson, H. (1893). *Poems*. Boston, MA: Roberts Brothers.

Johnson, S. (1982). *Inside an egg*. Minneapolis, MN: Lerner.

Johnson, S. (1989). *Silkworms*. Minneapolis, MN: Lerner.

Keller, E. F. (1983). *A feeling for the organism: The life and work of Barbara McClintock*. New York, NY: W. H. Freeman.

Kimmel, Eric A. (1988). *Anansi and the moss-covered rock*. New York, NY: Holiday House.

Lewis, C. S. (1956). *Surprised by joy; the shape of my early life*. New York, NY: Harcourt Brace.

Markandaya, K. (1954). *Nectar in a sieve*. New York, NY: J. Day.

Martin, A. (1985). Back to kindergarten basics. *Harvard Educational Review, 55*(3), 318–320.

McKie, R., & Eastman, P. D. (1962). *Snow*. New York, NY: Beginner Books.

Miller, E., & Almon, J. (2009). *Crisis in the kindergarten: Why children need to play in school*. College Park, MD: Alliance for Childhood.

Morrison, T. (1987). *Beloved*. New York, NY: Knopf.

Mosel, A. (1968). *Tikki Tikki Tembo*. Chicago, IL: Holt, Rinehart & Winston.

Naidoo, B. (1985). *Journey to Jo'burg: A South African story*. New York NY: J.B. Lippincott.

Napoli, D. J. (1992). *The prince of the pond*. New York, NY: Dutton Books.

National Council of Teachers of Mathematics. (2000). *Principles and standards for school mathematics*. Reston, VA: National Council of Teachers of Mathematics.

Paul, P. (2010, August 22). The littlest redshirts sit out kindergarten. *New York Times*. Retrieved from http://www.nytimes.com.

Paulsen, G. (1987). *Hatchet*. New York, NY: Bradbury Press.

Penrose, R. (1989). *The emperor's new mind: Concerning computers, minds, and the laws of physics*. New York, NY: Oxford University Press.

Randolph, V. (1976) *Pissing in the snow and other Ozark folktales*. Urbana: University of Illinois Press.

Richardson, K. (2003). *Assessing math concepts*. Bellingham, WA: Mathematical Perspectives.

Ringgold, F. (1991). *Tar Beach*. New York, NY: Crown.

Rosenblatt, L. M. (1989). *Literature as exploration*. New York, NY: Penguin Books.

Russell, S. J., Economopoulos, K., Tierney, C., Berle-Carman, M., Akers, J., Clements, D.H., . . . McMillen, S. (2004). *Investigations in number, data, and space*. Glenview, IL: Scott Foresman.

Santiago, E. (1994). *When I was Puerto Rican*. New York, NY: Vintage Books.

Selsam, M. (1987). *Egg to chick*. New York, NY: Harper & Row.

Shanker, A. (1995, December 3). What's new? *New York Times*. Retrieved from http://source.nysut.org/weblink7/DocView.aspx?id=1000

Shedlin, A. (1988, May). How about a national report card month? *Principal, 67*(5), 34.

Strieb, L. (2010). *Inviting families into the classroom: Learning from a life in teaching*. New York, NY: Teachers College Press.

Stroud, B. (2005). *The patchwork path: A quilt map to freedom*. Somerville, MA: Candlewick Press.

Taylor, M. D. (1976). *Roll of thunder, hear my cry*. New York, NY: Dial Press.

Temple, F. (1992). *Taste of salt: A story of modern Haiti*. New York, NY: Orchard Books.

Thompson, J. (1987). *Understanding teenagers' reading: Reading processes and the teaching of literature*. Norwood, SA: Australian Association for the Teaching of English.

U.S. National Commission on Excellence in Education. (1983). *A nation at risk: The imperative for educational reform*. Washington, DC: Author.

Vermont State Department of Education. (1971). *The Vermont design for education*. Montpelier, VT: Author (Original work published 1968).

Wagner, J. (1998). *Star Wars: Boba Fett—Death, lies, & treachery.* Milwaukie, OR: Dark Horse Comics.

Weber, L. (1997). *Looking back and thinking forward: Reexaminations of teaching and schooling.* New York, NY: Teachers College Press.

Weston, C. (1993). *Girltalk.* London, United Kingdom: Pan Macmillan.

Williams, R. (1961). *The long revolution.* New York, NY: Columbia University Press.

Yep, L. (1992). *Dragon war.* New York, NY: HarperCollins.

Zinn, Howard. (1980). *A people's history of the United States.* New York, NY: HarperCollins.

Index

About the Authors

Karen Bushnell, now retired, worked for the School District of Philadelphia for 23 years. Of all her jobs there, her favorite was classroom teacher.

Ann Caren worked as an elementary teacher and an instructional specialist in the Ithaca City School District for 36 years. She also served as a New York state consultant to teachers on young children's mathematical thinking. She had a long association with Prospect and served as President of Prospect's Board of Trustees from 2006 to 2010.

Patricia F. Carini is a cofounder of the Prospect School and Prospect Archives and Center for Education and Research. She began the Collections of Children's Works at Prospect and was instrumental in developing many of Prospect's professional development offerings. She has spoken and written widely on education and democratic values.

Kiran Chaudhuri has taught in New York City public schools for 22 years. She currently teaches English at Harvest Collegiate High School in Manhattan.

Louisa Cruz-Acosta is a retired bilingual and Reading Recovery teacher who taught for 25 years at the River East Elementary School and the Muscota New School/PS 314 in New York City, where she was a founding member of the faculty. Prior to this, she established bilingual education programs for adjudicated youth.

Peg Howes has taught 3rd and 4th grades in an upstate New York public school district for 18 years and has also been a K–8 enrichment teacher. Previously, she worked in several school districts in Vermont and taught 11- to 14-year-olds at Prospect School in North Bennington, VT. Peg is a graduate of Prospect's teacher education program.

Rhoda Kanevsky taught in the School District of Philadelphia for 33 years, 28 of those years at the Powel School. She currently is an instructor for graduate students in Reading/Writing/Literacy at the University of Pennsylvania.

Anne C. Martin, now retired, taught in public elementary schools for more than 30 years in New York City, London, and Brookline, MA. She has published numerous articles, as well as monographs about early education and the teaching of writing.

Betsy Nolan has taught in public schools for 25 years in Mamaroneck, NY. Her teaching career began in New York City, where she worked for the Christian Brothers and for the archdiocesan schools.

Chris Powers has been teaching in the School District of Philadelphia for 10 years. He is currently teaching 4th grade at Samuel Powel Elementary School, his neighborhood school.

Regina Ritscher taught elementary school for more than 20 years in a variety of settings and also taught aspiring teachers at Johnson State College in Vermont. She runs a small dairy farm and creamery and serves as a math specialist for River Rock School, a progressive independent school founded by a former Prospect teacher.

Ellen Schwartz taught in the public schools of Vermont and Massachusetts for 29 years, mainly teaching 3rd grade. She is a participant in an inquiry group rooted in Prospect's practices and a mentor to practitioner fellows working with the Prospect Archives at the University of Vermont.

Steve Shreefter worked in the New York City public school system from 1979 to 2007. He taught special education, American history and government, and literacy and designed and ran libraries in two different alternative high schools. From 2007 to 2011, Steve taught at the Long Island University School of Education, Brooklyn Campus, where he established a resource center for new teachers. Steve died in January 2013.

Lynne Yermanock Strieb taught 1st- and 2nd-graders in the School District of Philadelphia for 30 years and for 1 year was a Fulbright Exchange Teacher at an infants school in England. After retiring from teaching, she wrote *Inviting Families into the Classroom: Learning from a Life in Teaching*. She currently speaks about parental involvement and gives workshops on making books with children.

Bruce Turnquist taught in elementary classrooms for more than 25 years. He now mentors aspiring teachers at the University of New Hampshire, where he serves as a lecturer in education. He was a long-time participant in Prospect's institutes and conferences and is the director of the Institutes on Descriptive Inquiry, which carry on the tradition of Prospect's Summer Institutes.

Katharine Walmsley began her teaching career as a 1st-grade and ELL teacher in Holyoke, MA. She currently teaches 2nd grade at Jackson Street Elementary School in Northampton, MA.

Francesca Weiss has worked as an elementary teacher, literacy coach, and administrator in the New York City public school system.

Betsy Wice has been teaching in the School District of Philadelphia since 1964, mainly as a reading specialist. She also serves as a mentor to graduate students in Reading/Writing/Literacy at the University of Pennsylvania.